NICOLE MALIK

of DeliciousEveryday.com

weeknight
ONE-POT
VEGAN
COOKING

75 Effortless Recipes with
Maximum Flavor and Minimal Cleanup

PAGE STREET
PUBLISHING CO.

PAGE STREET
PUBLISHING CO.

Distributed by Macmillan, sales in Canada by The Canadian Manda Group.

23   22   21   20   19   1   2   3   4   5

ISBN-13: 978-1-62414-995-5

ISBN-10: 1-62414-995-2

Library of Congress Control Number: 2019940365

Cover and book design by Kylie Alexander for Page Street Publishing Co.

Photography by Nicole Malik

Printed and bound in the United States

dedication

To everyone trying to eat more kindly. Whatever your reason—whether you do it for yourself, for the world or for the animals—every little bite counts. You inspire me. And I hope these recipes inspire you.

table of CONTENTS

INTRODUCTION

I grew up in a time when meatless options were slim. It was normal to be offered a bowl of iceberg lettuce as a vegetarian entree at restaurants, and the word "vegan" was nowhere in the public vernacular. I'm so glad those days are long gone. I promise that every recipe here is delicious, real food. You won't find any salads or tofu in this book!

And best of all, every recipe is designed to be made in a single pot or pan, so you can get an incredible plant-based meal on the table without a ton of hassle and without spending the rest of the night cleaning the kitchen.

These are satisfying dishes that anyone will enjoy—whether you're a full-time vegan, an aspiring vegetarian or just looking to incorporate more meatless meals into your routine. In fact, I'm the only vegetarian in my family, and no one ever complains about the food!

So, how exactly did this cookbook—and my love of plant-based cooking—come to be?

Well, I was always a huge animal lover. And when I was twelve years old, I announced that I was now a vegetarian. My parents said it was great, surely thinking the idea would pass in a few days. Nearly 25 years later, I guess the joke is on them!

But I certainly didn't start out as an expert. As a young adult, I had the cooking skills of a llama—they don't cook, right? I couldn't even boil water without burning something. And I eventually realized that if I wanted to eat great food for the rest of my life, I'd need to learn to make it myself. So, I did.

I became a serious foodie, learning all there was to know about vegan cooking and nutrition, and serving up new meatless creations on the regular. And eventually, I started sharing them with my amazing readers on DeliciousEveryday.com. My little food blog has grown larger than I ever imagined, now providing cooking inspiration to nearly two million people every year.

These days, I'm a busy mom and businesswoman. While I still love cooking, I simply don't have hours to spend in the kitchen. And I certainly don't want to spend hours cleaning it up! So, these one-pot vegan meals were born.

These dishes are not overly fancy or complicated, but they are delicious and approachable. This is simply *good food* that you can *feel good* about eating.

I hope you and your family enjoy these recipes as much I enjoyed creating them.

Nicole Malik

GRAB THE BONUS CONTENT

Visit DeliciousEveryday.com/OnePotVeganBonus to grab some extra resources that I created just to complement this cookbook. You'll find vegan-friendly product recommendations, bonus recipes and handy printable cheat sheets to make vegan cooking easier than ever.

eat
YOUR
VEGGIES

If you're looking to spice up your dinner routine, this is the place to start.

Veggies are the star of the show in this chapter! From the Hoisin-Glazed Stuffed Acorn Squash (page 10) to the Roasted Tahini Eggplant Skewers (page 22) to the Portobello "Pot Roast" (page 21), these are the dishes that will finally inspire you to eat all those veggies.

These one-pot meals are packed with creative flavors borrowed from my favorite cuisines from all around the world. They're fun, flavorful and fit for a vegan foodie. Despite the big flavors, these dishes are all simple to prepare. You won't find any fussy ingredients or complex instructions. Just delicious, flavor-packed meals that you can cook up in a single pot or pan.

hoisin-glazed STUFFED ACORN SQUASH

SERVES
2

These acorn squash look incredibly impressive, but this is one of the easiest recipes in this whole cookbook! Simply mix the chickpea stuffing and hoisin glaze in a big bowl, stuff your acorn squash and roast to perfection. You won't believe how flavorful this is. This recipe is perfect for a romantic date night—or double it and invite the kids.

1 acorn squash, halved and seeds removed

Olive oil cooking spray

1 (15-oz [425-g]) can chickpeas, drained and rinsed

¼ cup (40 g) chopped red onion

2 scallions, sliced, greens and whites separated

⅓ cup (10 g) chopped spinach

⅓ cup (80 ml) hoisin sauce

1 tbsp (15 ml) soy sauce

1 tbsp (15 ml) rice vinegar

2 cloves garlic, minced

1 tsp ginger paste (see note)

Preheat the oven to 375°F (190°C, or gas mark 5).

Place the acorn squash in a baking dish, cut sides up. Spray the squash lightly with the olive oil cooking spray. Bake the squash for 20 minutes.

In a large mixing bowl, combine the chickpeas, red onion, scallion whites, spinach, hoisin sauce, soy sauce, rice vinegar, garlic and ginger paste.

Remove the acorn squash from the oven. Stuff the hollowed-out centers of each half with the chickpea filling. Gently brush some of the hoisin glaze from the stuffing over the exposed flesh of the squash. Return the squash to the oven and bake for 25 minutes, until it is tender.

Serve the squash topped with scallion greens.

note: Ginger is a flavor I love, and it makes an appearance in many of my dishes. I keep a tube of ginger paste in the fridge at all times. It tastes just like fresh ginger but is easier to use and keeps longer. If you prefer, you can substitute fresh minced ginger in any recipe that calls for ginger paste. A teaspoon of fresh minced ginger is equivalent to a teaspoon of ginger paste.

3-bean SOUTHWEST CORNBREAD PIE

**SERVES
6**

This cornbread pie is layered with flavor. A protein-packed three-bean filling, infused with Southwest spices and topped with sweet, golden cornbread. Yum! No one will believe you made this with a single skillet in less than 30 minutes.

FILLING

Olive oil cooking spray

1 (15-oz [425-g]) can black beans, drained and rinsed

1 (15.5-oz [439-g]) can kidney beans, drained and rinsed

1 (15.5-oz [439-g]) can cannellini beans, drained and rinsed

¼ cup (45 g) pimento-stuffed green olives, chopped

1 cup (154 g) fresh or frozen corn kernels

1 (14.5-oz [411-g]) can diced tomatoes

1 tsp chili powder

1 tsp curry powder

½ tsp smoked paprika

¼ tsp salt

⅛ tsp black pepper

CORNBREAD TOPPING

1 cup (159 g) cornmeal

1 cup (125 g) all-purpose flour

¾ cup (177 ml) almond milk

⅔ cup (126 g) sugar

1 tbsp (14 g) baking powder

½ tsp salt

FOR SERVING (OPTIONAL)

2 scallions, sliced

1 jalapeño, sliced

Preheat the oven to 425°F (220°C, or gas mark 7).

To make the filling, coat an ovenproof skillet in olive oil cooking spray. In the skillet, combine the black beans, kidney beans, cannellini beans, green olives, corn, tomatoes, chili powder, curry powder, smoked paprika, salt and pepper. Stir to combine the ingredients.

To make the topping, in a mixing bowl, combine the cornmeal, flour, almond milk, sugar, baking powder and salt. Mix until a smooth batter is formed. Gently spread the cornbread batter over the top of the bean mixture.

Bake for 15 to 20 minutes, or until the cornbread layer is slightly golden and the filling is warmed through.

Serve topped with scallions and jalapeño slices (if using).

crispy BLACK BEAN CHILAQUILES

**SERVES
4**

Loaded with black beans and crunchy fried tortillas, these chilaquiles are just as much fun to make as they are to eat. This is one of my favorite recipes for a fun family night in! It's so simple that your kids can help make it. And it cooks up in a single pan, making kitchen cleanup a breeze.

⅓–½ cup (80–120 ml) olive oil, divided

8 corn tortillas

1 tsp chipotle paste

3 cloves garlic, minced

1 yellow onion, chopped

1 cup (136 g) frozen corn kernels

2 red bell peppers, seeded and chopped

1 jalapeño pepper, seeded and chopped (optional)

¼ tsp chili powder

½ tsp ground coriander

1 tsp ground cumin

1 tbsp (3 g) finely chopped fresh oregano

2 (15-oz [425-g]) cans black beans, drained and rinsed

½ tsp salt, plus more to taste

⅛ tsp black pepper, plus more to taste

Juice of 1 lime

1½ cups (270 g) canned diced tomatoes

¼ cup (10 g) chopped fresh parsley (optional)

Have paper towels ready. Heat 2 tablespoons (30 ml) of the olive oil in a high-sided oven-safe pan over medium-high heat until hot but not smoking. Add one corn tortilla and fry it for 30 to 45 seconds. Flip the tortilla over and fry it for 30 to 45 seconds, until crispy. Set the cooked tortilla aside on a paper towel.

Repeat this process for all the tortillas, adding additional olive oil to the pan as needed. As the pan becomes hotter, each tortilla may take a bit less time to cook. Watch the tortillas carefully during this process, as times can vary depending on the exact temperature of your oil. Your finished tortillas should be crispy and golden in color, but not burned.

Drain the used frying oil from the pan and return the pan to the heat. Add 1 tablespoon (15 ml) of olive oil.

Add the chipotle paste, garlic and onion. Cook, stirring occasionally, for 2 to 3 minutes. Add the corn, bell peppers, jalapeño (if using), chili powder, coriander, cumin and oregano. Cook for 4 to 5 minutes, until the peppers are softened.

Add the black beans, salt, pepper and lime juice. Stir to combine. Stir in the tomatoes. Cover and cook over medium-low heat for 5 minutes. Season with salt and pepper, to taste. Remove the pan from the heat and set aside.

Break the fried tortillas into bite-sized pieces. On each plate, scatter a layer of tortilla pieces. Then top with a scoop of the black bean mixture. Then repeat for a second layer of tortilla pieces and a second layer of black beans. Garnish each dish with parsley (if using).

whole roasted
CAULIFLOWER IN KOREAN BARBECUE SAUCE

This cauliflower head is basted in a sweet and spicy Korean barbecue sauce and roasted until it's perfectly tender. It's incredibly delicious, insanely easy to prepare and looks like you worked on it all day! One cauliflower head is the perfect size for two. If you're feeding the whole family, double the recipe or serve it with rice or couscous.

¾ cup (165 g) packed brown sugar

1 cup (236 ml) soy sauce

2 tbsp (30 ml) rice wine vinegar

1 tbsp (21 g) harissa paste (see note)

1 tsp sesame oil

½ tsp black pepper

1 tsp ginger paste

2 cloves garlic, minced

1 tbsp (8 g) cornstarch

1 medium-sized head of cauliflower

2 scallions, sliced

1 tbsp (10 g) sesame seeds

Preheat the oven to 400°F (200°C, or gas mark 7).

Heat a large skillet over medium-high heat.

Add the brown sugar, soy sauce, rice wine vinegar, harissa paste, sesame oil, pepper, ginger paste and garlic. Whisk the sauce together and bring it to a bubble. Add the cornstarch and whisk until smooth.

Remove the skillet from the heat. Add the cauliflower head to the skillet and spoon over the sauce until the cauliflower is fully covered.

Place the skillet into the oven and roast the cauliflower for 30 to 35 minutes. Occasionally use a brush to baste the sauce over the cauliflower head. It's done when the cauliflower is fork tender.

Serve sprinkled with scallions and sesame seeds.

note: Harissa paste is a chili pepper–based paste, and it adds a great depth of flavor. If you have trouble finding it, feel free to substitute 1 tablespoon (15 ml) of your favorite chili-based hot sauce, such as Sriracha.

spinach, white bean &
SUN-DRIED TOMATO GRATIN

**SERVES
6**

This easy weeknight gratin might just be the best casserole you've ever made. The sun-dried tomatoes pack an intense punch of flavor, the white beans add a decadent creaminess and the fresh spinach adds a dose of nutritious protein. The whole dish is finished with a crispy, golden breadcrumb topping for a satisfying crunch. Just try not to eat the whole thing yourself.

2 tbsp (30 ml) olive oil, divided

½ yellow onion, thinly sliced

1 tsp salt, divided

2 cloves garlic, minced

2 tbsp (5 g) chopped fresh rosemary

1 tbsp (3 g) chopped fresh oregano

1 (8.5-oz [240-g]) jar oil-packed sun-dried tomatoes, drained and sliced

¼ cup (60 ml) vegetable broth

1 tbsp (15 ml) white wine vinegar

2 (15.5-oz [439-g]) cans cannellini beans, drained and rinsed

2 cups (60 g) fresh spinach leaves, roughly chopped

1 cup (125 g) panko breadcrumbs

1 tbsp (15 ml) lemon juice

¼ tsp black pepper

Chopped fresh basil

Preheat the oven to 375°F (190°C, or gas mark 5).

Heat 1 tablespoon (15 ml) of the olive oil in a large, ovenproof skillet over medium heat. Add the onion and ½ teaspoon of the salt. Cook for 5 to 6 minutes, stirring frequently, until the onion is just slightly browned.

Add the garlic, rosemary, oregano, sun-dried tomatoes, vegetable broth and white wine vinegar. Cook for 3 to 4 minutes, until the vinegar has mostly evaporated. Add the beans and spinach. Stir and cook for 2 minutes, until the spinach is wilted.

In a separate small mixing bowl, combine the breadcrumbs, 1 tablespoon (15 ml) of olive oil, lemon juice, ½ teaspoon of salt and the pepper.

Spread the breadcrumb mixture over the top of the casserole. Bake in the oven for 10 to 15 minutes, until the breadcrumb topping is golden brown. Serve topped with basil.

portobello "POT ROAST"

We all know the best part of a traditional pot roast is those roasted veggies, right? So, I've created a vegan version that delivers all of those familiar flavors in a completely plant-based, one-pot meal. While the veggies take a while to roast, there's only about ten minutes of active cooking time needed to pull off this impressive dish!

2 tbsp (30 ml) olive oil

2 yellow onions, sliced

4 cloves garlic, minced

6 tbsp (46 g) all-purpose flour

3 cups (708 ml) stout beer or other dark beer, such as porter

3 cups (708 ml) vegetable broth

¼ cup (60 ml) vegan Worcestershire sauce (see note)

¼ cup (66 g) tomato paste

2 tbsp (5 g) fresh sage, slivered

¼ cup (10 g) chopped fresh basil

2 tbsp (5 g) chopped fresh rosemary

Salt, to taste

Black pepper, to taste

4 portobello mushroom caps, stems and gills removed

2 cups (300 g) baby carrots

10 Yukon Gold potatoes, unpeeled and chopped into 1-inch (2.5-cm) pieces

Fresh rosemary sprigs (optional)

Preheat the oven to 350°F (175°C, or gas mark 4).

Heat the olive oil in a very large, ovenproof skillet over medium heat. Add the onions and garlic, and cook for 3 to 4 minutes. Add the flour to make a roux, stirring frequently for 1 minute. Slowly add the beer and vegetable broth to make a sauce.

Add the Worcestershire sauce, tomato paste, sage, basil, rosemary, salt and pepper. Add the portobellos, carrots and potatoes. Use a spoon to coat the vegetables with the sauce.

Transfer the skillet to the oven. Roast for 1 hour, or until the vegetables are tender. Serve with sprigs of rosemary for garnish (if using).

> ***note:*** Be sure to choose a vegan variety of Worcestershire sauce. Annie's and The Wizard's are both reliable brands.

roasted TAHINI EGGPLANT SKEWERS

SERVES 4

Eggplant is the star in these flavor-packed skewers! It's slathered in a creamy tahini dressing and roasted to perfection. And the best part? There's hardly any work involved here. Just mix the dressing, baste the eggplant slices and sit back while they roast.

½ cup (120 ml) tahini

⅔ cup (160 ml) coconut milk

¼ cup (60 ml) soy sauce

Juice of 1 lime

1 tbsp (14 g) minced fresh ginger

2 tbsp (30 ml) sesame oil

¾ cup (30 g) chopped fresh cilantro, divided

2 medium eggplants

Preheat the oven to 350°F (175°C, or gas mark 4).

Combine the tahini, coconut milk, soy sauce, lime juice, ginger, sesame oil and ½ cup (20 g) of cilantro in a small bowl. Whisk until it forms a cohesive sauce.

Slice the eggplants into ½-inch (1-cm) rounds, and arrange them on skewers. Place them onto a large baking sheet. Brush the eggplants generously with the tahini sauce, reserving ½ cup (120 ml) of the sauce for serving.

Bake the eggplant for 30 minutes, or until it is soft and tender. Serve with the remaining cilantro and the reserved tahini sauce, for dipping.

bonus: Make your own homemade tahini! Roast 1½ cups (120 g) of hulled sesame seeds at 350°F (175°C, or gas mark 4) for 7 minutes. Process in a blender or food processor with a pinch of salt and 1 to 2 tablespoons (15 to 30 ml) of canola oil.

family-style VEGGIE POTPIE

Individual veggie potpies are one of my favorite recipes to make for special occasions. But they can be a lot of work to put together. So, I've packed all the same flavor into a single pot with this family-style veggie potpie. Tender roasted veggies are cooked in a creamy broth, then wrapped in a perfectly flaky crust and baked to a golden finish.

SERVES
4

2 tbsp (30 ml) olive oil, divided

1 large onion, chopped

1 jalapeño pepper, seeded and minced

5 carrots, peeled and diced

2 cups (132 g) sliced white button mushrooms

¼ tsp salt

⅛ tsp black pepper

2 tbsp (5 g) chopped fresh thyme

3 tbsp (8 g) chopped fresh rosemary

3 cloves garlic, minced

1 tsp paprika

¼ tsp chili powder

3 tbsp (23 g) all-purpose flour

2 (15.5-oz [439-g]) cans cannellini beans, drained and rinsed

1 cup (154 g) fresh or frozen corn kernels

1 cup (150 g) fresh or frozen peas

5 cups (1.2 L) vegetable broth

½ cup (120 ml) almond milk

9 oz (225 g) frozen pie crust, thawed (see note)

Preheat the oven to 350°F (175°C, or gas mark 4).

Heat 1 tablespoon (15 ml) of olive oil in a deep, ovenproof skillet over medium heat. Add the onion and jalapeño, and cook for 2 to 3 minutes. Add the carrots and cook for 5 minutes, until softened. Add the mushrooms and cook for 3 to 4 minutes. Add 1 tablespoon (15 ml) of olive oil, salt, pepper, thyme, rosemary, garlic, paprika and chili powder. Stir. Add the flour and cook for 1 minute.

Add the beans, corn, peas and vegetable broth. Bring the mixture to a boil. Reduce to a simmer and cook, covered, for 10 to 15 minutes, until slightly reduced.

Stir in the almond milk and remove the skillet from the heat. Allow to cool until safe enough to handle.

Gently spread the pie crust over the top of the skillet, pressing down on the edges to seal. If the pie crust is much larger than your skillet, you may trim the edges so they extend about ½ inch (1.25 cm) beyond the edges of the pan. Cut several small slits in the top of the pie crust with a sharp knife. Bake for 20 to 25 minutes, until golden and flaky.

note: Be sure to use a vegan brand of pie crust. I particularly love Wewalka!

roasted SPRING RATATOUILLE

This unconventional ratatouille is a great way to show off your farmers' market haul! It features a fun mix of springtime veggies and a brightly flavored mustard vinaigrette, rather than a traditional tomato-based sauce. Experiment with your own favorite combination of veggies—use whatever is in season near you!

3 tbsp (45 ml) balsamic vinegar

2 cloves garlic, minced

1 tsp Dijon mustard

2 tbsp (30 ml) olive oil

1 tsp chopped fresh thyme

1 zucchini, sliced

1 yellow squash, sliced

1 red bell pepper, sliced

15 stalks asparagus, trimmed

½ red onion, sliced

1½ cups (188 g) trimmed and chopped green beans

½ pint (149 g) cherry tomatoes

1 cup (100 g) Brussels sprouts, halved

½ cup (62 g) breadcrumbs

Preheat the oven to 400°F (200°C, or gas mark 6).

In a large mixing bowl, combine the balsamic vinegar, garlic, Dijon mustard, olive oil and thyme. Add the zucchini, yellow squash, bell pepper, asparagus, red onion, green beans, tomatoes and Brussels sprouts to the bowl. Toss to coat with the dressing.

Spread the vegetables on a large baking sheet. Roast for 30 to 35 minutes, until tender. Remove the baking sheet from the oven and toss the vegetables with the breadcrumbs.

Turn on the broiler. Place the baking sheet under the boiler for 1 to 2 minutes, until the breadcrumbs are just crispy.

sheet-pan
SESAME GARLIC TEMPEH

SERVES
4

Tempeh is a nutrient-rich food made from soybeans. It has a nutty flavor and firm texture, and it is great at absorbing flavor from sauces and marinades. If you love the idea of tofu, but can't stand the mushy texture, you just might love tempeh! Coated in sesame garlic sauce and tossed with crispy roasted broccoli, it's lip-smacking good—and incredibly good for you.

2 tbsp (30 ml) sesame oil

4 cloves garlic, minced

2 tbsp (30 ml) rice wine vinegar

¼ cup (60 ml) agave syrup

⅓ cup (80 ml) sweet chili sauce

6 tbsp (98 g) tomato paste

¼ cup (55 g) packed brown sugar

2 (8-oz [226-g]) packages tempeh, cut into 1-inch (2.5-cm) cubes

4 cups (284 g) broccoli florets

3 tbsp (30 g) sesame seeds

Preheat the oven to 375°F (190°C, or gas mark 5).

In a large bowl, mix together the sesame oil, garlic, rice wine vinegar, agave syrup, sweet chili sauce, tomato paste and brown sugar. Add the tempeh and broccoli to the bowl, and toss to coat well.

Spread the tempeh and broccoli in a single layer on a large baking sheet. Bake for 20 minutes. Sprinkle with the sesame seeds and serve.

twice-baked
HARISSA-STUFFED POTATOES

SERVES
4

Twice-baked potatoes have always been one of my favorite treats. But preparing them always feels like so much work! So, for this easy version, I've amped up the flavor with spicy harissa and simplified the process to cook the potatoes from start to finish in a single pan. Don't be turned off by the long cook time—most of it is just waiting for the potatoes to bake!

4 large sweet potatoes

6 tsp (30 ml) olive oil, divided

2 tsp (10 g) salt, divided, plus more to taste

8 tsp (56 g) harissa paste

2 cups (472 g) plain dairy-free yogurt

Black pepper, to taste

2 scallions, sliced

Preheat the oven to 425°F (220°C, or gas mark 7).

Wash the sweet potatoes and use a fork to poke holes all over each potato. Rub the outside of each potato with ½ teaspoon of olive oil and ½ teaspoon of salt. Arrange the potatoes on a baking sheet and bake for 1 hour. The potatoes are done when they are fork tender.

Remove the potatoes from the oven and allow them to cool until they can be safely handled. Carefully slice off the top of each potato lengthwise. Then use a fork to gently mash the inside of each potato, being careful to keep the skin intact.

To each potato, add 2 teaspoons (14 g) of harissa paste, 1 teaspoon of olive oil, ½ cup (120 ml) of dairy-free yogurt, salt and pepper. Mash the mixture together with the potato flesh using the back of a fork.

Return the potatoes to the oven and bake for 10 minutes. Serve topped with scallions.

> *cheat:* If you are short on time, you can cook the potatoes in the microwave, stuff them and then finish them in the oven for 10 minutes!

panfried POLENTA PUTTANESCA

Puttanesca is a flavorful Italian sauce made with tomatoes, olive oil, olives and capers. It's traditionally served over pasta, but we're mixing it up and serving it atop lightly fried polenta slices, another Italian favorite. We keep the cooking simple and the cleanup easy by preparing both the polenta and the sauce in a single pan.

SERVES
4

2 tbsp (30 ml) olive oil, divided

8 slices tubed polenta (½-inch [1-cm]-thick slices)

Salt, to taste

Black pepper, to taste

½ yellow onion, chopped

2 cloves garlic, minced

3 tbsp (45 ml) balsamic vinegar

2 tbsp (32 g) tomato paste

1 tbsp (12 g) sugar

¼ tsp dried oregano

8 oz (226 g) baby portobello mushrooms, sliced

¼ cup (45 g) Kalamata olives, pitted and sliced

¼ cup (45 g) pimento-stuffed green olives, sliced

¾ cup (135 g) crushed tomatoes

1 (14.5-oz [411-g]) can diced fire-roasted tomatoes

Chopped fresh parsley

Heat 1 tablespoon (15 ml) of olive oil over medium-high heat in a nonstick pan. When the pan is hot, arrange the polenta slices in a single layer. You may need to work in batches if your pan is not large enough to fit all of the polenta slices.

Sprinkle the polenta with salt and pepper. Cook for 4 to 5 minutes. Flip the polenta slices over. Cook for 3 to 4 minutes, until the polenta is a light, golden brown. Remove the polenta slices from the pan and set aside.

In the same pan, heat 1 tablespoon (15 ml) of olive oil. Add the onion and garlic and cook for 4 to 5 minutes.

Add the balsamic vinegar, tomato paste, salt, pepper, sugar and oregano. Cook for 3 to 4 minutes. Add the mushrooms and olives. Cook for 5 minutes, until the mushrooms are softened. Add the crushed tomatoes and diced tomatoes. Simmer for 25 minutes, until the sauce is very thick.

Serve the polenta topped with puttanesca sauce and parsley.

fun fact: Puttanesca sauce is rumored to be the invention of Italian … ahem … ladies of the night. Hence its name, which roughly translates to "in the style of a prostitute." I have no idea if this is a true fact, but it sure makes for a fun story at dinnertime.

pumpkin & BLACK BEAN ENCHILADAS

SERVES
3

Enchiladas makes for a fun and easy weeknight meal. Just mix the pumpkin and black bean filling in one big bowl, roll the enchiladas and bake. You can even prep these ahead of time and pop them in the oven when you're ready for dinner. It doesn't get much easier than that.

Olive oil cooking spray

1 (14.5-oz [411-g]) can diced tomatoes

1 (15-oz [425-g]) can black beans, drained and rinsed

1 (15-oz [425-g]) can pumpkin puree

3 tbsp (15 g) taco seasoning

6 (8-inch [20-cm]) flour tortillas

1½ cups (354 ml) enchilada sauce

1 avocado, peeled, pitted and diced

¼ cup (10 g) chopped fresh cilantro

Sliced jalapeño pepper (optional)

Preheat the oven to 350°F (175°C, or gas mark 4). Spray a 9 x 13-inch (23 x 33-cm) baking dish lightly with olive oil cooking spray.

In a mixing bowl, combine the tomatoes, black beans, pumpkin puree and taco seasoning.

Lay a flour tortilla on a flat surface. Spoon approximately one-sixth of the filling down the center of the tortilla. Gently roll the tortilla around the filling. Place it seam side down in the baking dish. Repeat with the remaining filling and tortillas.

Pour the enchilada sauce over the tortillas. Bake for 20 minutes. Serve topped with avocado, cilantro and jalapeño (if using).

note: You will likely have extra filling. Feel free to make additional enchiladas if they fit in your baking dish. The filling also makes a great topping for mashed potatoes or a filling for pumpkin quesadillas.

EGGPLANT VERACRUZ

Veracruz is both a Mexican city and a traditional Mexican preparation for seafood. It consists of a tomato-based sauce flavored with olives, garlic and spices. We give fresh, tender eggplant the Veracruz treatment in this creative vegan meal. Even my eggplant-hating husband asked for seconds of this one!

SERVES
4

1 tbsp (15 ml) olive oil

1 yellow onion, thinly sliced

2 cloves garlic, minced

½ cup (120 ml) white wine, such as Chardonnay

1 eggplant, sliced into ¼-inch (6-mm)-thick half-moons

½ cup (33 g) sliced baby portobello mushrooms

¼ cup (65 g) jarred diced pimentos

¼ cup (45 g) green olives, sliced

½ tsp dried oregano

Salt, to taste

Black pepper, to taste

1 (14.5-oz [411-g]) can diced tomatoes

FOR SERVING (OPTIONAL)

Crusty bread

Fresh parsley

Heat the olive oil in a large skillet over medium-high heat. Add the onion and garlic and cook for 3 to 4 minutes. Add the white wine and cook for 1 to 2 minutes. Add the eggplant, mushrooms, pimentos, green olives and oregano. Add the salt and pepper. Cook for 4 to 5 minutes, until the mushrooms and eggplant are softened.

Add the tomatoes and bring the mixture to a boil. Reduce it to a simmer and cook for 10 to 15 minutes, until the eggplant is tender.

Serve with a crusty bread and garnish with parsley (if using).

bang-bang CAULIFLOWER BITES

SERVES 4

These crispy little cauliflower bites are so good, you won't be able to stop popping them! They're marinated in a sweet chili sauce, then coated with a crispy panko coating to give them the perfect bit of crunch. These are great on their own as a light meal, or make a whole tray for a party appetizer.

½ cup (120 ml) sweet chili sauce

¼ cup (60 ml) Sriracha sauce

2 tsp (10 ml) agave syrup

Juice of 2 limes

4 cloves garlic, minced

Salt, to taste

Black pepper, to taste

4 cups (284 g) cauliflower florets

6 tbsp (46 g) panko breadcrumbs

Chopped fresh parsley (optional)

Preheat the oven to 425°F (220°C, or gas mark 7).

In a large bowl, whisk together the sweet chili sauce, Sriracha sauce, agave syrup, lime juice, garlic, salt and pepper.

Toss the cauliflower florets in the marinade. Spread them out on a baking sheet in a single layer and bake for 20 minutes. Remove the pan from the oven and sprinkle the cauliflower bites with panko breadcrumbs.

Return the pan to the oven and bake for 5 to 7 minutes, until crispy. Garnish with parsley (if using).

orange-balsamic glazed
BUTTERNUT SQUASH &
BRUSSELS SPROUTS

The sweet cranberries and crunchy almonds contrast with the tangy orange-balsamic glaze in this flavorful dish. It's delicious and simple to prepare in a single baking dish. It's also pretty enough to serve to guests. In fact, this is one of my go-to dishes for Thanksgiving each year! You can easily double or even triple this recipe if you're feeding a crowd.

4 cups (400 g) Brussels sprouts, trimmed and halved

3 cups (420 g) peeled and diced butternut squash (1-inch [2.5-cm] cubes)

¼ cup (60 ml) olive oil

¼ tsp salt, plus more to taste

⅛ tsp black pepper

3 tbsp (45 ml) agave syrup

3 tbsp (45 ml) balsamic vinegar

⅔ cup (160 ml) orange juice

1 cup (125 g) almonds

½ cup (83 g) dried cranberries

Preheat the oven to 425°F (220°C, or gas mark 7).

In a large baking dish, combine the Brussels sprouts and butternut squash. Drizzle the olive oil over the vegetables. Add the salt and pepper.

Toss the vegetables to coat them in the olive oil, then place the baking dish in the oven and roast for 40 minutes.

When the vegetables are done, remove the baking dish from the oven. Add the agave syrup, balsamic vinegar and orange juice. Toss the vegetables so they are fully coated in the glaze. Return the dish to the oven and bake for 5 to 10 minutes, until the vegetables are soft and slightly caramelized.

Remove the baking dish from the oven again. Add additional salt, to taste. Stir in the almonds and dried cranberries just before serving.

herbed
CORN FRITTERS WITH TOMATO-AVOCADO SALSA

SERVES
3

These delightful corn fritters are simple to prep and cook up in a single skillet in just fifteen minutes. This makes for a refreshing lunch or a light dinner—perfect for hot summer nights!

TOMATO-AVOCADO SALSA

3 cups (450 g) roughly chopped cherry tomatoes

2 tsp (10 ml) white wine vinegar

Salt, to taste

Black pepper, to taste

2 tbsp (30 ml) olive oil

2 avocados, peeled, pitted and diced

CORN FRITTERS

4 cups (636 g) cornmeal

1½ cups (188 g) all-purpose flour

2 cups (472 ml) almond milk

2 tbsp (28 g) baking powder

½ cup (77 g) fresh or frozen corn kernels

½ tsp dried oregano

½ tsp garlic

½ tsp thyme

2 tbsp (30 ml) olive oil

3-4 cups (708-944 ml) canola oil, for frying

To make the salsa, in a small bowl, mix together the tomatoes, white wine vinegar, salt, pepper and olive oil. Set aside.

To make the fritters, in a medium bowl, mix together the cornmeal, flour, almond milk, baking powder, corn, oregano, garlic, thyme and olive oil.

Form the batter into pancake-shaped fritters, roughly 3 inches (7.5 cm) in diameter. You should get at least six fritters from your batter.

Heat the canola oil in a large deep-sided skillet over medium-high heat. When the oil is very hot, add the corn fritters. (The oil is hot enough when a few drops of water added to the skillet create a sizzle.) Cook the fritters for 3 to 5 minutes, until golden brown, turning halfway through.

Mix the avocados into the salsa, tossing them to coat them in the dressing. Arrange the corn fritters on a serving dish and top with tomato-avocado salsa.

note: Try topping these corn fritters with a dollop of vegan sour cream, or your own favorite salsa—mango or pineapple salsa would be delicious.

eat with YOUR HANDS

There's something that's just so fun about eating with your hands! Just ask any kid.

But these irresistible finger foods were created with the grown-ups in mind. Each one is hearty enough to serve for dinner, brimming with unique flavors and incredibly fun to eat.

This chapter is full of family-friendly options, such as Chickpea Burgers with Sweet Mustard Sauce (page 46), Asian Skillet Nachos with Wasabi Crema (page 49) and 15-Minute Falafel with Tahini-Lemon Dipping Sauce (page 65). Plus, there are a few decidedly grown-up treats, such as Samosa Summer Rolls (page 57) and Fig & Balsamic Skillet Flatbread (page 61). And the Street Corn Pita Pockets (page 53) make for a great packable lunch.

True to my promise, each one of these dishes can be prepared in a single pot or pan—so you won't need to spend your evening cleaning up the kitchen. And since you're eating with your hands, you can even skip the serving dishes and utensils too. Did I mention I hate doing dishes?

So, go ahead, get your fingers dirty!

chickpea burgers with
SWEET MUSTARD SAUCE

SERVES
4

Who doesn't love a great veggie burger? These chickpea burgers are a quick and hearty meal that will please the entire family, kids included. They're made from protein-rich chickpeas and topped with a sweet and tangy mustard sauce for an extra dose of flavor.

CHICKPEA BURGERS

½ yellow onion, finely diced

2 (15.5-oz [439-g]) cans chickpeas, drained and rinsed

¼ cup (10 g) finely chopped fresh cilantro

½ tsp adobo seasoning

¼ tsp paprika

Salt, to taste

Black pepper, to taste

3 tbsp (23 g) all-purpose flour

3 tbsp (45 ml) olive oil, divided

SWEET MUSTARD SAUCE

1 tbsp (15 ml) agave syrup

2 tbsp (30 ml) Dijon mustard

FOR SERVING

4 burger buns

Lettuce

Red onions, thinly sliced

Alfalfa sprouts

To make the burgers, in a large bowl, mix the onion, chickpeas, cilantro, adobo seasoning, paprika, salt, pepper, flour and 1 tablespoon (15 ml) of olive oil. Mash everything together well with a potato masher, then stir to combine. The mixture will be thick and slightly firm, like cookie dough. You can also complete this step in a food processor, if you prefer.

Form the mixture into four large patties.

Heat the remaining 2 tablespoons (30 ml) of olive oil in a large nonstick pan over medium heat. Arrange the burger patties in a single layer. Cook for 4 to 5 minutes on each side, until the patties are heated through.

To make the sauce, in a small bowl, mix together the agave syrup and Dijon mustard.

Serve each burger on a bun, topped with lettuce, red onions, alfalfa sprouts and a drizzle of the sweet mustard sauce.

asian
SKILLET NACHOS WITH WASABI CREMA

As a kid, one of my all-time favorite treats was getting to have nachos for dinner. This grown-up version elevates nachos to a whole new level with Chinese-spiced veggies and a spicy wasabi-yogurt sauce. It makes an incredibly fun and simple weeknight dinner. You can easily scale this recipe up or down—the only limit is the size of your pan.

SKILLET NACHOS

1 tbsp (15 ml) sesame oil

2 cups (132 g) sliced mushrooms

½ yellow onion, sliced

½ green bell pepper, sliced

2 tbsp (30 ml) soy sauce

1 tsp Chinese five-spice powder

1 (6-oz [170-g]) package tortilla chips

WASABI CREMA

¼ cup (60 g) plain dairy-free yogurt

½ tsp wasabi paste

FOR SERVING

½ cup (35 g) shredded cabbage

½ cup (50 g) shredded carrots

2 scallions, sliced

Preheat the oven to 425°F (220°C, or gas mark 7).

To make the nachos, heat the sesame oil in an oven-safe skillet over medium-high heat. Cook the mushrooms, onion and bell pepper for 6 to 7 minutes, until softened. Add the soy sauce and Chinese five-spice powder, and cook for another 1 to 2 minutes. Remove the vegetables from the pan and set aside.

To make the wasabi crema, mix the dairy-free yogurt and wasabi paste in a small bowl and set aside.

Arrange the tortilla chips in the skillet. Top the chips with the cooked vegetables. Bake for 5 minutes, until just warmed. Top with the shredded cabbage, carrots, scallions and wasabi crema.

mushroom
TINGA TACOS

SERVES
4

This plant-based take on traditional tinga uses fresh mushrooms for a hearty and delicious filling. They're simmered in a smoky, slightly spicy tomato sauce and served up taco-style so we can eat with our hands!

2 tbsp (30 ml) olive oil

1 yellow onion, finely diced

3 cloves garlic, minced

2 cups (132 g) sliced mushrooms

1 (14.5-oz [411-g]) can diced fire-roasted tomatoes

1 tbsp (15 ml) adobo sauce, from canned chipotle peppers

1 tsp cumin

1 tsp dried oregano

Salt, to taste

Black pepper, to taste

8 corn tortillas

FOR SERVING
Plain dairy-free yogurt

Chopped fresh cilantro

Chopped red onion

Lime wedges

Heat the olive oil in a large skillet over medium heat. Add the onion and cook for 4 to 5 minutes. Add the garlic and mushrooms and cook for 5 to 6 minutes, until softened.

Add the tomatoes and adobo sauce, gently mashing as you add them to the pan. Add the cumin, oregano, salt and pepper. Allow the mixture to come to a bubble, then reduce the heat and simmer for 5 to 10 minutes.

Top each tortilla with one-eighth of the mushroom mixture and fold in half to form the tacos. Serve the tacos topped with dairy-free yogurt, cilantro, red onion and lime wedges.

note: Add additional adobo sauce for a spicier dish, or omit it entirely to keep things nice and mild.

street corn PITA POCKETS

These pita pockets were inspired by Mexican street corn, a popular and totally delicious street food. In this quick and easy version, we roast our corn on a single sheet pan, toss it with a creamy dairy-free yogurt and stuff it into pita pockets for a yummy sandwich!

1 onion, chopped

1 jalapeño pepper, seeded and chopped

4 cloves garlic, peeled and minced

4 cups (616 g) fresh or frozen corn kernels

1 tsp chili powder

½ tsp salt

¼ tsp black pepper

2 tbsp (30 ml) olive oil

2 tbsp (30 g) plain dairy-free yogurt

Juice of 1 lime

4 pieces pita bread, sliced in half

1 cup (40 g) roughly chopped lettuce (any variety)

½ cup (20 g) roughly chopped fresh parsley

4 radishes, thinly sliced

Preheat the oven to 400°F (200°C, or gas mark 6).

On a large baking sheet, spread the onion, jalapeño, garlic and corn in a single layer. Add the chili powder, salt, pepper and olive oil. Toss to coat all the vegetables in the spices.

Roast the corn for 20 minutes. Remove the baking sheet from the oven. Toss the corn mixture with the dairy-free yogurt and lime juice.

Stuff each pita bread half with one-eighth of the corn mixture. Add the lettuce, parsley and radishes to the pita pockets and serve.

note: For a protein-packed sandwich, try adding some black beans or chickpeas to the corn mixture during the final 5 minutes of roasting.

loaded black bean
BURRITOS WITH SRIRACHA-YOGURT SAUCE

SERVES
4

Burritos make for a really simple, crowd-pleasing meal. In this easy version, we wrap up healthy black beans and delicious guacamole with a homemade spicy "yogurt" sauce. Then we toast it to perfection on the stovetop. There's hardly any prep work and the whole meal is ready in just twenty minutes.

SRIRACHA-YOGURT SAUCE

1 cup (236 g) plain dairy-free yogurt (see note)

3 tbsp (45 ml) Sriracha sauce or similar hot sauce

2 tbsp (30 ml) lime juice

HOMEMADE GUACAMOLE (OPTIONAL)

4 avocados, peeled and pitted

½ cup (90 g) chopped fresh tomato

½ cup (80 g) chopped red onion

Juice of 1 lime

Salt, to taste

Black pepper, to taste

BLACK BEAN BURRITOS

4 (12-inch [30-cm]) flour tortillas

2 cups (300 g) guacamole, homemade or store-bought

2 (15-oz [425-g]) cans black beans, drained and rinsed

1½ cups (231 g) fresh corn kernels

½ cup (20 g) chopped fresh cilantro

Salt, to taste

Black pepper, to taste

To make the sauce, in a small bowl, combine the dairy-free yogurt, Sriracha sauce and lime juice. Set aside.

To make the homemade guacamole (if using), mash together the avocados, tomato, red onion, lime juice, salt and pepper in a medium bowl. Set it aside.

To make the burritos, lay the tortillas on a clean surface. Spread 2 tablespoons (30 g) of the yogurt sauce down the center of each tortilla.

Down the center of each tortilla and on top of the sauce, spread a line of the guacamole, black beans, corn and cilantro. Sprinkle with salt and pepper. Fold in two sides of the tortilla, and then roll it up tightly to seal the fillings inside the tortilla.

Heat a nonstick skillet over medium heat. Arrange the burritos seam side down in the pan. Cover the pan and cook for 8 to 10 minutes, until lightly toasted and warm throughout. Work in two batches if all of the burritos don't fit in your pan.

Serve the burritos with the remaining Sriracha-yogurt sauce.

note: I typically use a soy-based dairy-free yogurt, but there are many variations available and you can use them interchangeably throughout these recipes. Cashew- or coconut milk–based yogurts work equally well.

SAMOSA SUMMER ROLLS

These creative summer rolls bring all the flavor of traditional Indian samosas. They're filling and easy to prep in a single pan. They're also an incredibly fun way to eat with your fingers! Don't forget the mint chutney—these morsels are just made for dipping.

SERVES
3

SUMMER ROLLS

3 tbsp (45 ml) olive oil, divided

½ onion, finely diced

3 cloves garlic, minced

3 small Yukon Gold potatoes, diced

⅓ cup (37 g) shredded carrots

½ cup (75 g) frozen peas

1 tsp garam masala

2 tsp (4 g) curry powder

½ tsp turmeric

¼ tsp salt

½ tsp cumin

⅛ tsp cayenne pepper (optional)

6 rice paper sheets

Dried cilantro (optional)

Mint chutney, homemade or store-bought

HOMEMADE MINT CHUTNEY (OPTIONAL)

1½ cups (60 g) fresh cilantro

½ cup (20 g) fresh mint

½ jalapeño pepper

⅓ cup (80 g) plain dairy-free yogurt

To make the summer rolls, heat 1 tablespoon (15 ml) of the olive oil in a large nonstick pan over medium heat. Add the onion and garlic, and cook for 3 to 4 minutes until soft and fragrant. Add the remaining 2 tablespoons (30 ml) of olive oil, the potatoes, carrots and peas. Cook for 2 minutes. Add the garam masala, curry powder, turmeric, salt, cumin and cayenne pepper (if using). Cook for 5 minutes. Cover and cook for 12 to 15 minutes, stirring occasionally, until the potatoes are soft. Remove the pan from the heat.

Soak a rice paper sheet in warm water for 5 seconds. Lay it on a flat surface and spread roughly one-sixth of the potato filling down the center. Roll the rice paper around the filling, as if you were rolling a burrito. Repeat for all six rolls.

To make the homemade mint chutney (if using), add the cilantro, mint, jalapeño and dairy-free yogurt to a blender. Process until the mixture is mostly smooth.

Garnish the samosa rolls with a sprinkle of dried cilantro (if using), and serve with the mint chutney for dipping.

smashed
AVOCADO QUESADILLAS

SERVES
4

If you love avocado, then you're going to love these quesadillas. Creamy, fresh avocado is layered with refried beans and sweet cherry tomatoes, then toasted up inside crispy quesadillas and dipped in a homemade chive-yogurt sauce. Delicious.

QUESADILLAS

2 avocados, peeled and pitted

Juice of 1 lime

½ tsp salt

¼ tsp black pepper

8 (10-inch [25-cm]) flour tortillas

2 cups (300 g) chopped cherry tomatoes

1 cup (200 g) vegan refried beans

Olive oil cooking spray

DIPPING SAUCE

1 cup (236 g) plain dairy-free yogurt

Juice of 1 lime

2 tbsp (6 g) chopped fresh chives

FOR SERVING

1 lime, cut into wedges

Fresh cilantro

To make the quesadillas, in a small bowl, mash together the avocado, lime juice, salt and pepper. Set aside.

Lay one tortilla on a flat surface. Spread the avocado mixture across half of the tortilla. Top it with cherry tomatoes. Spread the refried beans across the other half of the tortilla. Fold it in half to make the quesadilla. Repeat this process with the remaining tortillas and fillings.

Spray a large nonstick pan with olive oil cooking spray. Heat it over medium-high heat. Place two quesadillas in the pan. Cook for 2 to 3 minutes on each side, until just golden brown. Repeat with the remaining quesadillas.

To make the dipping sauce, in a small serving dish, mix together the dairy-free yogurt, lime juice and chives.

Serve the quesadillas with the dipping sauce, lime wedges and cilantro.

> *note:* Try adding corn, black beans or even pomegranate seeds for a fun new twist on these quesadillas.

fig & balsamic
SKILLET FLATBREAD

SERVES
2

This flatbread is full of amazing flavor from subtly sweet figs, caramelized onions and a sticky balsamic glaze. It's really fun to watch the dough cook up in a big skillet on the stovetop, and the hot pan gives the flatbread a perfectly crunchy crust. One flatbread is the perfect size for two—but you can make several if you're feeding a crowd.

HOMEMADE PIZZA DOUGH (OPTIONAL)

2 cups (250 g) all-purpose flour, plus more if needed

1½ tsp (8 g) sugar

½ tsp salt

2½ tsp (10 g or 1 packet) instant yeast

¼ tsp garlic

¾ cup (177 ml) water

1–2 tbsp (15–30 ml) olive oil, if needed

SKILLET FLATBREAD

1 tbsp (15 ml) olive oil

½ yellow onion, sliced

½ lb (226 g) fresh pizza dough, homemade or store-bought

1 cup (166 g) sliced dried figs

1 cup (40 g) arugula

2 tbsp (30 ml) balsamic glaze, homemade or store-bought

1 tbsp (15 ml) agave syrup

HOMEMADE BALSAMIC GLAZE (OPTIONAL)

1 cup (236 ml) balsamic vinegar

To make the homemade pizza dough (if using), mix together the flour, sugar, salt, instant yeast, garlic and water. If the dough is too dry, add 1 to 2 tablespoons (15 to 30 ml) of olive oil. If it's too wet, sprinkle in additional flour as needed. Knead until the ingredients are well combined and a cohesive dough has formed. Set the dough aside to rise for at least 1 hour.

To make the flatbread, heat the olive oil over medium heat in a 10-inch (25-cm) skillet. Add the onion and cook for 8 to 10 minutes, until slightly caramelized. Remove the onion from the pan and set the pan aside.

Roll out the pizza dough to roughly ¼ inch (6 mm) thick and 12 inches (30 cm) around. Carefully press the pizza dough into the skillet and return it to the heat. Cook for 4 to 5 minutes. Flip the dough and cook for 5 to 6 minutes, until the crust is cooked through and slightly crispy. Remove the skillet from the heat.

To make the homemade balsamic glaze (if using), heat the balsamic vinegar in a small nonstick pot over medium-high heat. Bring it to a boil, then reduce the heat and simmer until the liquid is reduced by about half, 5 to 7 minutes.

Top the flatbread with the dried figs, onions and arugula. Drizzle with the balsamic glaze and agave syrup.

note: Balsamic glaze can be found near the vinegars in most grocery stores. It's simply balsamic vinegar reduced into a sticky syrup. You can purchase it or make the homemade version included above.

white bean &
TOMATO BRUSCHETTA

This hearty bruschetta makes for a light, satisfying meal. Creamy cannellini beans are paired with fresh tomatoes, artichokes and black olives and served over perfectly toasted French bread. A few slices of this loaded bruschetta will be enough to fill even the hungriest bellies.

SERVES
4

12 large (1-inch [2.5-cm]) slices French bread

2 (15.5-oz [439-g]) cans cannellini beans, drained and rinsed

4 cloves garlic, minced

2 tsp (10 ml) lemon juice

1 tsp salt, divided

2 pints (596 g) cherry tomatoes, halved

2 (14-oz [397-g]) cans artichoke hearts, drained and chopped

½ cup (90 g) black olives, sliced

½ cup (120 ml) olive oil

2 tbsp (30 ml) balsamic vinegar

¼ tsp black pepper

FOR SERVING
Fresh parsley

Fresh basil

Preheat the oven to 375°F (190°C, or gas mark 5).

Arrange the bread slices on a large baking sheet. In a small bowl, mash together the beans, garlic, lemon juice and ¼ teaspoon of the salt. Spread the mixture onto the slices of bread.

In a mixing bowl, combine the tomatoes, artichoke hearts, black olives, olive oil, balsamic vinegar, the remaining salt and the pepper.

Spread the tomato mixture on top of the bread slices. Bake for 10 minutes, until the bread is slightly toasted and the toppings are warm. Serve the bruschetta topped with parsley and basil.

15-minute
FALAFEL WITH TAHINI-LEMON DIPPING SAUCE

**SERVES
2**

Falafel—the hero of Greek food! Seriously, who doesn't love falafel? This crazy easy homemade version is fun, fast and flavorful. It's perfect dipped in tangy tahini-lemon sauce.

DIPPING SAUCE

¼ cup (60 g) tahini

3 tbsp (45 ml) lemon juice

2 tbsp (30 ml) olive oil

2 tbsp (30 g) plain dairy-free yogurt

Salt, to taste

Black pepper, to taste

FALAFEL

2 (15.5-oz [439-g]) cans chickpeas, drained and rinsed

2 cloves garlic, minced

2 shallots, finely chopped

¼ cup (10 g) finely chopped fresh parsley

½ tsp dried oregano

½ tsp salt

⅛ tsp black pepper

2 tbsp (16 g) all-purpose flour

3 tbsp (45 ml) olive oil

3-4 cups (708–944 ml) canola oil, for frying

FOR SERVING

Fresh parsley

Pita bread

To make the dipping sauce, in a small bowl, mix together the tahini, lemon juice, olive oil, dairy-free yogurt, salt and pepper. Set it aside.

To make the falafel, combine the chickpeas, garlic, shallots, parsley, oregano, salt, pepper, flour and olive oil in a large bowl, mashing the chickpeas with a fork or potato masher. You can also combine the ingredients in a food processor, if you prefer.

Roll the falafel batter into eight to ten large patties, approximately 1½ inches (3.5 cm) wide.

Place a large deep-sided skillet over medium heat. Fill the pan with the canola oil, and heat the oil. Place the falafel patties into the hot frying oil, so they are completely submerged. Cook for 3 to 5 minutes, until the falafel patties are golden brown.

Serve the falafel with the dipping sauce, parsley and pita bread.

sizzling
SKILLET FAJITAS WITH CILANTRO-JALAPEÑO SAUCE

SERVES
4

These fajitas are full of Southwestern spice and served piping hot from the skillet over warm tortillas. Then they're drizzled with a homemade cilantro-jalapeño sauce. Yum! Best of all, you can have them ready in just twenty minutes.

SKILLET FAJITAS

8 (10-inch [25-cm]) flour tortillas

2 tbsp (30 ml) olive oil

2 yellow onions, sliced

2 red bell peppers, seeded and sliced

2 green bell peppers, seeded and sliced

4 cups (264 g) sliced baby portobello mushrooms

½ tsp chili powder

1 tsp smoked paprika

1 tsp garlic powder

1 tsp ground cumin

1 tsp salt

½ tsp black pepper

Lime wedges

CILANTRO-JALAPEÑO SAUCE

2 cups (472 g) plain dairy-free yogurt

2 cups (80 g) chopped fresh cilantro

1 jalapeño pepper, seeded

1 tsp salt

Black pepper, to taste

Juice of 2 limes

To make the fajitas, heat the oven to 350°F (175°C, or gas mark 4). Wrap the tortillas in a piece of aluminum foil, and place them in the oven to warm while you cook.

Heat the olive oil in a large cast-iron pan over medium-high heat. Add the onions and bell peppers. Cook for 4 to 6 minutes, until they are tender and slightly charred. Add the mushrooms, chili powder, smoked paprika, garlic powder, cumin, salt and pepper. Cook for 5 to 7 minutes, until the mushrooms are softened and slightly caramelized.

To make the sauce, in a blender or food processor, combine the dairy-free yogurt, cilantro, jalapeño, salt, pepper and lime juice. Puree the mixture into a smooth sauce.

Top each warm tortilla with the cooked vegetables, a squeeze of lime and a drizzle of the cilantro-jalapeño sauce.

jamaican jerk
VEGGIE & PINEAPPLE LETTUCE WRAPS

SERVES
4

These colorful lettuce wraps are every bit as delicious as they are pretty. The intense pineapple flavor is a perfect complement for the jerk seasoning and roasted veggies. These wraps make for a fun and easy family dinner. And the best part is that you get to eat them with your hands! So, you know the kids will be on board.

2 red bell peppers, sliced

1 red onion, sliced

1 cup (66 g) sliced mushrooms

1 cup (71 g) broccoli florets (chopped into bite-sized pieces)

2 tbsp (30 ml) olive oil

½ tsp salt

¼ tsp black pepper

2 tbsp (10 g) jerk seasoning

1 cup (165 g) chopped pineapple

DIPPING SAUCE
½ cup (120 g) plain dairy-free yogurt

1 tsp dried cilantro

Juice of ½ lime

Salt, to taste

Black pepper, to taste

FOR SERVING
8 large lettuce leaves

Lime wedges

Dried cilantro

Preheat the oven to 425°F (220°C, or gas mark 7).

Toss the bell peppers, red onion, mushrooms and broccoli on a sheet pan with the olive oil, salt, pepper and jerk seasoning. Roast the vegetables in the oven for 20 to 25 minutes, until they are tender. Remove the vegetables from the oven and toss them with the pineapple.

To make the dipping sauce, in a small bowl, mix the dairy-free yogurt, cilantro, lime juice, salt and pepper.

Serve the vegetables with lettuce for wrapping and a squeeze of fresh lime juice. Garnish the lettuce wraps with additional dried cilantro.

note: Try replacing the pineapple with papaya or mango for a fun variation.

crowd-pleasing
COMFORT FOOD

There's something so comforting about a big bowl of noodles, isn't there? And growing up in an Italian family, I certainly got my share.

I've taken some of the most beloved pasta dishes and re-invented them as new plant-based versions. You'd never guess that there's not an ounce of dairy in my creamy Linguini with Roasted Red Pepper Alfredo (page 96) or cheesy Grown-Up Jalapeño Mac and Cheese (page 80). And even my Italian grandmother wouldn't miss the meat in the hearty Penne with Mushroom Bolognese (page 72).

But we don't stop with the classics! I've also included some surprising new flavor combinations, such as Fiery Red Curry Noodles (page 76) and Mango Tango Pesto Pasta (page 87), that will give your old comfort foods a run for their money.

If you're looking for surefire dishes that will please even the pickiest eaters in your family, these easy one-pot pastas and risottos are a great place to start. And, of course, every one of these dishes cooks up in a single pot or pan, so the cleanup is just as simple as the cooking.

penne with MUSHROOM BOLOGNESE

SERVES
4

My mushroom Bolognese has been a long-time favorite of readers (and me) for years. But I don't always have the time to pull it all together. So, I created this quick one-pot version that can be on the table in under 30 minutes. I think it's even tastier than my original recipe, as the pasta cooks directly in the sauce, soaking up tons of flavor!

2 tbsp (30 ml) olive oil

1 onion, diced

2 medium carrots, shredded

3 cloves garlic, minced

1 tsp dried thyme

¼ tsp crushed red pepper flakes

16 oz (454 g) baby portobello mushrooms, diced finely

1 cup (236 ml) red wine, such as Cabernet Sauvignon

2 cups (472 ml) vegetable broth

2 tbsp (30 ml) soy sauce

1 (14.5-oz [411-g]) can diced tomatoes

1 cup (180 g) crushed tomatoes

1 tbsp (16 g) tomato paste

1 (16-oz [454-g]) box penne pasta

Salt, to taste

Black pepper, to taste

FOR SERVING (OPTIONAL)
Fresh basil

Dairy-free Parmesan cheese shreds

Heat the olive oil in a large stockpot over medium heat. Add the onion and carrots, and cook for 3 to 4 minutes. Add the garlic, thyme, red pepper flakes and mushrooms. Cook for 5 to 6 minutes, until the mushrooms are softened.

Add the red wine, vegetable broth, soy sauce, diced tomatoes, crushed tomatoes and tomato paste. Bring the mixture to a boil.

Add the pasta. Cover the pot and cook for 12 to 14 minutes, stirring occasionally, until the pasta is tender and the sauce is thickened.

Season with salt and pepper, to taste. Serve topped with basil and dairy-free Parmesan cheese (if using).

creamy
PUMPKIN RISOTTO WITH FRIED SAGE

SERVES
4

Every year when the weather turns cold, I start to cook pumpkin everything! It's like a sign that the holidays are on their way. This pumpkin risotto is everything a good risotto should be—comforting, creamy and completely indulgent. We top it with fried sage leaves, pepitas and dried cranberries for a slightly sweet and satisfyingly crunchy finish.

1 tsp plus 1 tbsp (23 ml) olive oil, divided

¼ cup (10 g) fresh sage leaves

½ onion, chopped

2 cloves garlic, minced

½ tsp cumin

½ tsp ginger paste

1 cup (210 g) Arborio rice

½ cup (120 ml) dry white wine, such as Chardonnay

4 cups (944 ml) vegetable broth, divided

1 cup (225 g) canned pumpkin puree

Salt, to taste

Black pepper, to taste

2 tsp (6 g) pepitas

2 tsp (7 g) dried cranberries

Heat 1 teaspoon of the olive oil in a large pot over high heat. Add the sage and fry it for 2 to 3 minutes, stirring occasionally, until crispy. Remove the sage from the pot and set it aside on a paper towel.

Heat 1 tablespoon (15 ml) of the olive oil in the same pot over medium heat. Add the onion and garlic, and cook for 3 to 4 minutes, until softened. Add the cumin and ginger paste. Cook for 1 minute. Stir in the rice and toast it for 1 minute, stirring continually. Add the white wine and cook for 3 to 4 minutes, until the wine is mostly absorbed.

Add 1 cup (236 ml) of vegetable broth to the pot. Simmer, stirring frequently, until most of the liquid is absorbed. Repeat this process, adding additional broth each time the liquid becomes absorbed, until all of the broth is incorporated. The full process of cooking the rice should take 25 to 30 minutes.

Stir in the pumpkin puree, salt and pepper. Cook for 3 to 4 minutes, until the mixture is heated through. Serve the risotto topped with fried sage leaves, pepitas and dried cranberries.

fiery RED CURRY NOODLES

SERVES
3

I first fell in love with Thai cuisine on my honeymoon in Krabi. I love the distinctive combination of sweet coconut milk, spicy curry, fresh ginger and lemongrass. Yum! I've brought together all of those intense flavors in this easy noodle dish. We use a quick-cooking ramen-style noodle to absorb all the incredible flavors.

2 tbsp (30 ml) olive oil

1 red bell pepper, thinly sliced

1 green bell pepper, thinly sliced

1 yellow onion, sliced

1½ cups (165 g) shredded carrots

1½ cups (147 g) snow peas

2 cloves garlic, minced

2 tbsp (28 g) peeled and chopped fresh ginger

1 tbsp (14 g) lemongrass paste

1 (13.5-oz [400-ml]) can coconut milk

2 tbsp (28 g) red curry paste

½ tsp crushed red pepper flakes, plus more for serving

2 cups (472 ml) vegetable broth

1 (8-oz [226-g]) package Chinese noodles (see note)

Salt, to taste

Black pepper, to taste

¼ cup (10 g) chopped fresh cilantro

Lime wedges

Heat the olive oil in a large wok over medium heat. Add the bell peppers and onion. Cook for 3 to 5 minutes, until the vegetables are softened. Add the carrots and snow peas. Cook for 3 to 5 minutes more.

Add the garlic, ginger and lemongrass paste. Cook for 1 to 2 minutes. Add the coconut milk, red curry paste and red pepper flakes. Stir the mixture well to combine. Cook for 5 minutes over medium heat.

Add the vegetable broth and bring the sauce to a boil. Stir in the noodles. Cook uncovered for 6 to 7 minutes, until the noodles are fully cooked and the sauce has thickened. Add salt and pepper, to taste.

Serve topped with cilantro and a lime wedge.

> *note:* Chinese noodles are thin, quick-cooking wheat-based noodles that absorb flavors very well. They are almost always vegan, but be sure to check the label. The KA•ME brand is a reliable choice. If you prefer, you can substitute traditional noodles, such as vermicelli.

stovetop
LASAGNA SKILLET

SERVES
6

Lasagna is one of those amazing foods that often gets relegated to special occasions because it takes so much time and effort to put together. This one-pan lasagna skillet brings all the flavor of traditional lasagna in an easy weeknight meal! I've even snuck in nutritious cannellini beans and lentils for a hidden punch of protein.

1 tbsp (15 ml) olive oil

½ onion, chopped

2 cloves garlic, minced

1 (14.5-oz [411-g]) can diced tomatoes with juices

1 (28-oz [794-g]) can crushed tomatoes

½ tsp dried oregano

½ tsp thyme

¼ tsp salt

¼ tsp crushed red pepper flakes

½ cup (120 ml) vegetable broth

⅓ cup (66 g) red lentils

1 (15.5-oz [439-g]) can cannellini beans, drained and rinsed

8 oz (227 g) no-bake lasagna noodles

Fresh parsley and/or basil (optional)

Heat the olive oil in a large, deep-sided skillet over medium heat. Add the onion and garlic. Cook for 3 to 4 minutes, until softened.

Add the diced tomatoes, crushed tomatoes, oregano, thyme, salt, red pepper flakes and vegetable broth. Bring to a boil, and stir in the lentils and cannellini beans. Add the lasagna noodles to the pan, breaking them into large pieces as needed to fit the pan. Stir to combine and submerge the noodles as much as possible.

Cover and simmer for 16 to 20 minutes, until the noodles are tender. Stir the noodles occasionally to keep the pasta from sticking together and to keep the noodles coated in tomato sauce.

Serve topped with fresh herbs (if using).

grown-up JALAPEÑO MAC AND CHEESE

SERVES
4

Who doesn't love mac and cheese? I've made so many versions over the years, searching for the perfect plant-based recipe. This one-pot dish is definitely the simplest, and cheesiest, one I've come up with yet! And I couldn't resist spicing things up with a bit of jalapeño—feel free to omit it for a more kid-friendly dish.

1 tbsp (15 ml) olive oil

2 jalapeño peppers, seeded and finely diced

2 cloves garlic, minced

3 cups (708 ml) vegetable broth

3 cups (708 ml) almond milk or other dairy-free milk

1 (16-oz [454-g]) box rotini pasta

2 cups (241 g) vegan Cheddar cheese shreds (see note)

Salt, to taste

Black pepper, to taste

1 jalapeño pepper, thinly sliced

Heat the olive oil in a large pot over medium-high heat. Add the diced jalapeño peppers and cook for 3 to 4 minutes, until softened, stirring frequently. Add the garlic and cook for 1 minute.

Add the vegetable broth and almond milk to the pot. Bring to a boil. Add the pasta and cook for 8 to 10 minutes.

Reduce the heat to low and slowly stir in the vegan cheese shreds, until it forms a creamy sauce. Add salt and pepper, to taste. Serve topped with sliced jalapeño.

note: Choose a brand of vegan cheese that melts well to get the most authentic "cheese" sauce! Some of my favorite brands are Daiya, Follow Your Heart and So Delicious.

sun-dried
TOMATO VODKA PENNE

Vodka with dinner? Yes, please! Classic vodka penne gets an upgrade in this new dish, infused with intense flavor from sun-dried tomatoes. This easy meal feels very fancy, but it's simple to prep in less than 30 minutes.

2 tbsp (30 ml) olive oil

1 small yellow onion, finely chopped

6 cloves garlic, minced

1 cup (236 ml) vodka

1 cup (240 g) oil-packed sun-dried tomatoes, drained

2 (28-oz [794-g]) cans diced tomatoes with juices

6 tbsp (98 g) tomato paste

1 tsp dried oregano

¼ cup (60 ml) balsamic vinegar

1 (16-oz [454-g]) box penne pasta

Fresh basil

Heat the olive oil in a large pot over medium-high heat. Add the onion and garlic, and cook for 2 minutes. Add the vodka and cook for 5 minutes. Add the sun-dried tomatoes, diced tomatoes, tomato paste, oregano and balsamic vinegar. Heat until the mixture comes to a bubble.

Add the pasta and cook for 12 minutes, or until pasta is tender. Serve topped with basil.

toasted
BROWN BUTTER GNOCCHI

Gnocchi (pronounced nyawk-kee) is one of my favorite foods in the entire world. I was lucky enough to visit Italy after graduation and spent the whole trip eating gnocchi at every restaurant I could find, in search of the very best ones. I found that gnocchi dishes went well beyond the traditional marinara sauce. This brown "butter" recipe is a vegan version of one of my favorites. And it's easy to make with just a handful of simple ingredients.

SERVES
4

1 (16-oz [454-g]) package potato gnocchi, refrigerated variety (see notes)

⅓ cup (75 g) vegan margarine (see notes)

3 tbsp (45 ml) balsamic vinegar

1½ cups (45 g) roughly chopped spinach

FOR SERVING (OPTIONAL)

Pine nuts

Fresh parsley

Fill a large stockpot with water and bring it to a boil. Cook the gnocchi until they float to the surface, about 4 to 5 minutes. Drain the water and set aside.

In the same pot, melt the vegan margarine over medium heat. Add the balsamic vinegar and stir. Add the cooked gnocchi to the pot and toss it with the brown butter sauce. Toast the gnocchi for 1 to 2 minutes, until they are just slightly golden.

Stir in the spinach leaves, until just wilted. Serve the gnocchi topped with pine nuts and parsley (if using).

notes: You can use any prepared gnocchi for this recipe. I prefer the refrigerated varieties, as they tend to be freshest. But you can also use dried gnocchi. Just be sure to adjust the cook time according to the package directions.

A good vegan margarine will produce the most realistic "butter" sauce. I like the Earth Balance brand. If you prefer, you can substitute extra virgin olive oil.

mango tango PESTO PASTA

SERVES
4

Mango and pesto? You're going to have to trust me on this one. It's a surprising flavor combination that just works. It's also a quick dinner recipe that you can get on the table in just fifteen minutes! If you're feeling ambitious, take a few extra minutes to make your own homemade pesto sauce too.

¼ cup (32 g) pine nuts

1 (16-oz [454-g]) box casarecce pasta or your favorite shape

2 cups (300 g) frozen peas

1 cup (236 ml) vegan pesto, homemade or store-bought

2 mangos, peeled and diced

Fresh basil

HOMEMADE VEGAN PESTO (OPTIONAL)

2 cups (80 g) fresh basil

⅔ cup (89 g) pine nuts

3 cloves garlic

½ cup (120 ml) olive oil

¼ tsp salt

⅛ tsp black pepper

1 tbsp (15 ml) lemon juice

Heat a large dry stockpot over medium heat. When the pan is hot, add the pine nuts and cook for 1 to 2 minutes, until just toasted. Remove the pine nuts from the pan and set them aside.

Fill the pot with water and bring it to a boil. Add the pasta and cook for 9 to 10 minutes, until tender. Add the peas and cook for 1 to 2 minutes. Drain the pasta and peas in a colander, and return them to the pot.

To make the homemade vegan pesto (if using), combine the basil, pine nuts, garlic, olive oil, salt, pepper and lemon juice in the blender. Process until smooth.

Mix the pesto sauce into the pasta. Toss with the mangos. Serve the pasta topped with toasted pine nuts and basil.

kickin'
CREAMY BROCCOLI PASTA

SERVES
4

Broccoli is my son's all-time favorite vegetable, and this one-pot pasta is a fun and tasty way to serve it. Crunchy broccoli florets contrast perfectly with the creamy garlic and red pepper sauce. It packs a surprising bit of spice—so go easy on the red pepper if you like things mild! This sauce is also a great base to experiment with. Try replacing the broccoli with your own favorite veggies, such as mushrooms or fresh peas, for a completely new dish.

3 tbsp (45 ml) olive oil, divided

6 cloves garlic, minced

2 shallots, chopped

4 cups (284 g) broccoli florets

Salt, to taste

½ tsp crushed red pepper flakes, plus more for serving

¼ cup (32 g) cornstarch

4 cups (944 ml) vegetable broth

2 cups (472 ml) almond milk

1 (16-oz [454-g]) box farfalle pasta

Fresh parsley

Heat 2 tablespoons (30 ml) of the olive oil in a large pot over medium-high heat. Add the garlic and shallots. Cook for 2 to 3 minutes. Add the broccoli, salt and red pepper flakes. Cook for 4 to 5 minutes, until the broccoli begins to soften.

Add the cornstarch and the remaining 1 tablespoon (15 ml) of olive oil. Cook, stirring continuously, for 1 minute. Add the vegetable broth and almond milk. Stir to combine.

Add the pasta and bring the mixture to a boil. Cover, then reduce the heat and simmer for 12 to 15 minutes, until the pasta is cooked and the sauce has thickened.

Serve with parsley and additional red pepper flakes, if desired.

note: Almond milk is my preferred substitute for traditional dairy milk. For the recipes in this book, you can use any plant-based milk that you prefer. Cashew milk, soy milk and rice milk are all excellent choices. Just be sure to choose an unsweetened and unflavored variety, unless otherwise noted.

mediterranean
LUNCHBOX PASTA

**SERVES
6**

Greece is one of my favorite places on Earth, particularly the Cyclades island of Naxos. This Mediterranean pasta was inspired by all of my favorite Greek flavors—sun-dried tomatoes, Kalamata olives, artichokes, capers and spicy pepperoncini peppers! I call this one "lunchbox pasta" because it's equally good served the next day as a cold pasta salad. This is my potluck go-to!

1 (16-oz [454-g]) box tri-color rotini pasta

1 (8.5-oz [240-g]) jar oil-packed sun-dried tomatoes, drained and julienned

1 (7-oz [196-g]) jar Kalamata olives, pitted and sliced

1 (14-oz [397-g]) can artichoke hearts, drained and chopped

2 tbsp (8 g) capers

¼ cup (43 g) chopped jarred pepperoncini peppers

2 tbsp (30 ml) olive oil

⅓ cup (13 g) chopped fresh parsley

Salt, to taste

Black pepper, to taste

Bring a large pot of water to a boil over medium-high heat. Add the pasta and cook for 10 to 12 minutes, until tender. Drain well.

In a large bowl, toss together the pasta, sun-dried tomatoes, Kalamata olives, artichoke hearts, capers, pepperoncini peppers, olive oil, parsley, salt and pepper.

note: Try experimenting with flavored olive oils to change up this easy dish!

herbed
AGLIO E OLIO

Aglio e Olio is a classic, simple Italian dish that's made even simpler in this one-pot version. Noodles are cooked in a garlicky broth for maximum flavor and tossed with garden-fresh herbs. And the best part is you can make it in just twenty minutes! Try experimenting with your favorite combination of herbs. Some delicious choices are cilantro, dill and even mint.

SERVES
4

¼ cup (60 ml) olive oil

10 cloves garlic, minced

8 cups (2 L) vegetable broth

1 (16-oz [454-g]) box spaghetti

½ tsp black pepper

2 cups (80 g) chopped fresh parsley

1 cup (40 g) chopped fresh basil

1 cup (48 g) chopped fresh chives

Heat the olive oil in a large pot over medium heat. Add the garlic and cook for 2 to 3 minutes, until it is fragrant and golden.

Add the vegetable broth and spaghetti to the pot. Bring it to a boil. Cook for 11 to 12 minutes, or until the pasta is tender and the liquid is mostly absorbed.

Add the pepper, parsley, basil and chives. Toss the pasta to mix it with the herbs.

truffled MUSHROOM RISOTTO

SERVES
3

Mushroom risotto is the ultimate comfort food—it's creamy, hearty and feels indulgent. This version doesn't disappoint. It's loaded with fresh mushrooms and herbs, and it's drizzled with decadent truffle oil. And it's ready to eat in under an hour!

1 tbsp (15 ml) olive oil

½ yellow onion, diced

2 cloves garlic, minced

¼ tsp dried tarragon

1 tsp chopped fresh parsley

1 tsp chopped fresh thyme

Salt, to taste

Black pepper, to taste

1½ cups (100 g) sliced baby portobello mushrooms

1 cup (210 g) Arborio rice

½ cup (120 ml) dry white wine, such as Chardonnay

4 cups (944 ml) vegetable broth, divided

FOR SERVING (OPTIONAL)
Fresh sage

2 tsp (10 ml) truffle oil

Heat the olive oil in a large pot over medium heat. Add the onion and garlic. Cook for 3 to 4 minutes, until softened. Add the tarragon, parsley, thyme, salt and pepper. Cook for 1 minute. Add the mushrooms. Sauté for 5 to 6 minutes, until they are softened.

Stir in the rice and toast it for 1 minute, stirring continually. Add the white wine. Cook for 3 to 4 minutes, until the wine is mostly absorbed.

Add 1 cup (236 ml) of the vegetable broth to the pot. Simmer, stirring frequently, until the liquid is absorbed. Repeat this process, adding additional broth each time the liquid becomes absorbed, until all the broth is incorporated. The full process of cooking the rice should take 25 to 30 minutes.

Serve the risotto topped with fresh sage and a drizzle of truffle oil (if using).

note: The truffle oil is completely optional, but highly recommended. It's one of those splurge ingredients that is totally worth keeping in the pantry. Try it drizzled over pizzas, flatbreads, bruschetta, ravioli or baked potatoes!

linguini with
ROASTED RED PEPPER ALFREDO

SERVES
4

This roasted red pepper Alfredo sauce has all the delicious creaminess of traditional Alfredo, with none of the dairy. And it's exploding with flavor from roasted red peppers and herbs. It looks and tastes like a gourmet meal but comes together in under 30 minutes.

1 (16-oz [454-g]) jar roasted red peppers, drained

1⅔ cups (392 ml) almond milk

¼ tsp crushed red pepper flakes

½ tsp dried oregano

¼ tsp salt

⅛ tsp black pepper

1 tbsp (15 ml) olive oil

2 shallots, minced

2 cloves garlic, minced

3 tbsp (24 g) cornstarch

¾ cup (177 ml) vegetable broth

1 (16-oz [454-g]) box linguini

¼ cup (10 g) chopped fresh parsley

2 tbsp (22 g) slivered almonds

In a blender, combine the roasted red peppers, almond milk, red pepper flakes, oregano, salt and pepper. Process until a smooth sauce forms. Set the sauce aside.

In a large pot, heat the olive oil over medium heat. Add the shallots and garlic, and cook for 2 minutes. Add the cornstarch and stir continuously for 30 seconds.

Add the roasted red pepper sauce and vegetable broth to the pot. Heat until the mixture comes to a bubble.

Add the linguini, ensuring all of the noodles are submerged in the sauce, and cover. Simmer for 12 to 14 minutes, until the pasta is cooked and the sauce is thickened. Stir occasionally to keep the pasta from sticking together.

Serve the pasta topped with parsley and slivered almonds.

cheat: It's worth pulling out the blender for this easy dish, but you can also finely dice the red peppers and sauté them along with the shallots and garlic. The sauce won't be quite as thick and cohesive, but it will still taste delicious.

greek-style ZUCCHINI-TOMATO ORZO

Orzo looks just like rice, but it's actually a pasta! This sneaky little pasta is particularly popular in Greek and Middle Eastern cuisine. Fresh zucchini and ripe tomatoes are sautéed to bring out their delicious flavors, then they are cooked into the creamy orzo and folded together with fresh arugula and herbs.

**SERVES
4**

2 tbsp (30 ml) olive oil

½ onion, chopped

1 zucchini, sliced into ¼-inch (6-mm) half-moons

1 cup (149 g) halved cherry tomatoes

2 cloves garlic, minced

2 cups (336 g) dry orzo

2 cups (472 ml) vegetable broth

1 cup (180 g) crushed tomatoes

½ cup (20 g) roughly chopped arugula

Salt, to taste

Black pepper, to taste

¼ cup (10 g) chopped fresh parsley

Heat the olive oil in a large pot over medium heat. Add the onion and cook for 3 minutes, until softened. Add the zucchini, cherry tomatoes and garlic. Cook for 7 to 8 minutes, until the vegetables are softened and slightly browned.

Add the orzo, and stir continuously for 1 minute. Add the vegetable broth and crushed tomatoes. Bring to a boil. Reduce the heat and simmer uncovered for 10 minutes, until the orzo is tender.

Stir in the arugula. Add salt and pepper, to taste. Sprinkle with fresh parsley before serving.

incredible GRAINS

As a mom, I'm always on the lookout for easy recipes that my family will eat—but I want to make sure they're getting nutritious food, too. So, I love to incorporate rice, grains and legumes into my cooking. These wholesome, versatile ingredients make a fantastic base for all kinds of one-pot creations. If you're looking for a simple meal that packs a healthy punch, this is the chapter for you.

But don't let the word "healthy" scare you off. These dishes deliver big on flavor as well. From the Spicy Mexican Quinoa Skillet (page 105) to the Louisiana-Style Cajun Jambalaya (page 113) to the dinner party–worthy Italian Stuffed Peppers (page 110), there's a little something for everyone.

spring
VEGETABLE PAELLA

SERVES
4

This vegan paella is bursting with Spanish flavor. The rice is simmered in a flavorful mixture of broth and white wine, then loaded up with fresh seasonal veggies. The saffron is a splurge ingredient that's worth the expense. Did you know it takes 75,000 saffron flowers to make just one pound of this unique spice? In this dish, it adds a brilliant color, aroma and distinct flavor that is the hallmark of traditional paella.

2 tbsp (30 ml) olive oil

1 red bell pepper, seeded and sliced

½ onion, chopped

½ fennel bulb, thinly sliced

1 clove garlic, minced

1 tsp dried thyme

1 tsp paprika

1 tsp salt

¼ tsp turmeric

½ tsp saffron threads

2 cups (420 g) Arborio rice

4½ cups (1.1 L) vegetable broth, divided

1 cup (236 ml) dry white wine, such as Chardonnay

½ lb (226 g) asparagus, trimmed

1 cup (150 g) fresh or frozen peas

1 (7.5-oz [212-g]) jar artichoke hearts, drained and sliced

1 (15.5-oz [439-g]) can cannellini beans, drained and rinsed

½ cup (24 g) chopped fresh chives (optional)

In a large nonstick pan, heat the oil over medium heat. Add the bell pepper, onion and fennel. Cook for 3 to 5 minutes, until softened. Add the garlic, thyme and paprika. Cook, stirring occasionally, for 2 minutes.

Stir in the salt, turmeric, saffron and rice. Add 3 cups (708 ml) of the vegetable broth and the wine. Bring the mixture to a boil. Continue cooking over medium-high heat, stirring often, for 5 minutes.

Once most of the broth has been absorbed by the rice, stir in the asparagus, peas, artichokes and beans. Add the remaining broth. Reduce the heat to low and simmer, covered, for 10 minutes, until the broth is mostly absorbed.

Remove the pan from the heat. Garnish with chives (if using).

spicy
MEXICAN QUINOA SKILLET

SERVES
4

Nutritious quinoa and black beans bring a double dose of protein to this Mexican-inspired dish. It's filled with hidden veggies that the kids will actually eat, and the creamy, heart-healthy avocado is the perfect match for the spicy jalapeños. The quinoa cooks right in the skillet, where it can soak up all of those incredible flavors. Feel free to double this recipe for your next fiesta!

2 tbsp (30 ml) olive oil

3 cloves garlic, minced

2 scallions, sliced, white and green parts separated

1–2 jalapeño peppers, seeded and minced

2 tsp (5 g) chili powder (omit for a less spicy dish)

2 tsp (5 g) cumin

1 tsp smoked paprika

1½ cups (255 g) dry quinoa

2½ cups (592 ml) vegetable broth

1 (15-oz [425-g]) can black beans, drained and rinsed

1 cup (154 g) fresh or frozen corn kernels

1 (14.5-oz [411-g]) can diced tomatoes

Salt, to taste

Black pepper, to taste

2 avocados, peeled, pitted and sliced

¼ cup (10 g) chopped fresh cilantro

Heat the olive oil in a large high-sided pan over medium heat. Add the garlic, scallion whites and jalapeños. Cook for 1 minute. Add the chili powder, cumin and smoked paprika.

Add the quinoa, vegetable broth, black beans, corn and tomatoes to the pan. Season with salt and pepper. Stir to combine.

Cover the pan with a lid and cook for 15 minutes. When cooked, fluff the quinoa with a fork. Add additional salt, to taste.

Serve topped with avocado slices, scallion greens and cilantro.

---

note: You'll know the quinoa is done when the little white "tails" appear.

---

red beans & rice WITH VEGGIE KEBABS

A little bit of creativity turns this elaborate-looking two-part dish into a simple one-pot meal. Skewers are filled with fresh veggies and tossed with smoky Cajun spice, then roasted right over top of the red beans and rice casserole.

KEBABS

½ red onion, cut into 1-inch (2.5-cm) chunks

1 yellow bell pepper, cut into 1-inch (2.5-cm) slices

1 zucchini, cut into 1-inch (2.5-cm)-thick half-moons

12 baby portobello mushrooms

Olive oil cooking spray

Salt, to taste

Black pepper, to taste

1 tsp blackened seasoning

RED BEANS & RICE

2 tbsp (30 ml) olive oil

½ yellow onion, chopped

2 cloves garlic, minced

½ jalapeño, seeded and finely chopped

1 green bell pepper, seeded and chopped

2 (15.5-oz [439-g]) cans red kidney beans, drained and rinsed

1 (28-oz [794-g]) can diced tomatoes

1 tsp blackened seasoning

Salt, to taste

Black pepper, to taste

1 cup (236 ml) vegetable broth

1 cup (210 g) long-grain rice

FOR SERVING (OPTIONAL)

¼ cup (10 g) chopped fresh cilantro

½ jalapeño pepper, sliced

Preheat the oven to 350°F (175°C, or gas mark 4).

To make the kebabs, arrange the red onion, bell pepper, zucchini and mushrooms on skewers. Spray the kebabs lightly with olive oil cooking spray. Sprinkle them with salt, pepper and blackened seasoning. Set aside.

To make the red beans and rice, heat the olive oil in a deep, ovenproof skillet over medium-high heat. Add the onion, garlic, jalapeño and bell pepper. Cook for 5 minutes, until the peppers are softened. Add the red kidney beans, tomatoes, blackened seasoning, salt, pepper and vegetable broth. Heat until the mixture comes to a bubble. Add the rice and simmer for 5 minutes.

Place the kebabs across the top of the pan, so they sit above the rice. Bake for 30 minutes, until the rice is cooked and the veggie kebabs are tender.

Season the beans and rice with salt and pepper, to taste. Serve topped with cilantro and jalapeño slices (if using).

cuban
LENTIL PICADILLO

This veggie-packed twist on traditional Cuban picadillo features hearty lentils and creamy golden potatoes loaded up with flavorful Cuban spices. The sweet raisins are a surprisingly perfect contrast to the salty capers and Spanish olives. Served with a crusty baguette, it makes for a filling one-pot meal.

2 tbsp (30 ml) olive oil

½ red onion, chopped

½ jalapeño, seeded and minced

Salt, to taste

Black pepper, to taste

½ cup (55 g) shredded carrots

2 small Yukon Gold potatoes, cubed

2 cloves garlic, minced

1 cup (236 ml) vegetable broth

1 cup (198 g) red lentils

1 (14.5-oz [411-g]) can diced tomatoes

2 tsp (5 g) cumin

1 tsp smoked paprika

1 tsp dried oregano

1 tbsp (15 ml) white wine vinegar

2 tbsp (8 g) capers

½ cup (90 g) Spanish olives with pimentos, sliced

⅓ cup (50 g) raisins

FOR SERVING
Sliced baguette

Fresh parsley

Heat the olive oil in a large pan over medium-high heat. Add the red onion, jalapeño, salt and pepper. Cook for 3 to 5 minutes, until the vegetables are softened. Add the carrots, potatoes and garlic. Cook for 5 minutes, stirring occasionally.

Add the vegetable broth, lentils, tomatoes, cumin, smoked paprika, oregano and white wine vinegar. Bring the mixture to a boil, then reduce the heat and simmer for 25 minutes.

Stir in the capers, olives and raisins. Serve with crusty baguette slices and fresh parsley.

note: For a more traditional take on this classic dish, serve with tortillas in place of the baguette.

italian
STUFFED PEPPERS

Stuffed peppers don't get any easier (or more gorgeous!) than this. Sweet roasted bell peppers are packed with a tasty rice-based filling, brimming with hearty flavor from fresh veggies, ripe tomatoes, crunchy walnuts and garden herbs. This recipe is so simple to make—yet pretty enough to serve to guests. Try putting a new twist on this dish by substituting couscous or quinoa for the rice.

2 tbsp (30 ml) olive oil

3 cloves garlic, minced

1 shallot, minced

½ tsp crushed red pepper flakes

1 bay leaf

1 tbsp (5 g) dried oregano

¼ tsp salt

⅛ tsp black pepper

1 zucchini, sliced into ½-inch (1-cm) pieces

1 yellow squash, sliced in ½-inch (1-cm) pieces

¼ cup (29 g) chopped walnuts

¼ cup (45 g) black olives, sliced

1 cup (180 g) canned fire-roasted diced tomatoes, drained

½ cup (90 g) canned crushed tomatoes

1 cup (236 ml) vegetable broth

1 cup (105 g) long-grain rice

4 red bell peppers

Olive oil cooking spray

¼ cup (31 g) panko breadcrumbs

Chopped fresh basil

Preheat the oven to 375°F (190°C, or gas mark 5).

Heat the olive oil over medium-high heat in a deep, ovenproof skillet. Add the garlic, shallot, red pepper flakes, bay leaf and oregano. Cook for 2 to 3 minutes, until fragrant.

Add the salt, pepper, zucchini and yellow squash. Cook for 4 to 5 minutes, until the vegetables are softened. Add the walnuts, black olives, diced tomatoes, crushed tomatoes and vegetable broth. Cook until the mixture begins to bubble. Add the rice. Reduce the heat and simmer for 15 minutes.

Slice the bell peppers in half lengthwise. Remove the seeds and discard. Spray the bell peppers lightly with olive oil spray.

Remove the bay leaf from the skillet. Scoop the rice mixture into the bell peppers, filling them completely. Remove leftover rice mixture from the pan, if there is any. Arrange the stuffed bell peppers in the same pan. Transfer the pan to the oven and bake for 25 minutes, or until the bell peppers are tender.

Top with the breadcrumbs and basil before serving.

louisiana-style
CAJUN JAMBALAYA

This one-pot jambalaya is full of nutritious veggies simmered in a Cajun-spiced tomato broth. This is an easy go-to weeknight meal that only takes 30 minutes to prepare. And it tastes so good, no one will even realize it's healthy. Feel free to experiment with your favorite combination of veggies! Try it with mushrooms, diced potato, asparagus, snap peas, pearl onions or whatever vegetables are in season near you.

SERVES 6

2 tbsp (30 ml) olive oil

1 red bell pepper, sliced

1 yellow bell pepper, sliced

1 yellow onion, diced

1 cup (125 g) trimmed green beans

1 cup (100 g) thinly sliced okra

2 cloves garlic, minced

½ jalapeño (or more to taste), seeded and finely diced

1 tbsp (5 g) Creole seasoning

Salt, to taste

Black pepper, to taste

1 (14.5-oz [411-g]) can diced tomatoes with juices

1 cup (180 g) crushed tomatoes

2 tbsp (30 ml) vegan Worcestershire sauce

3 cups (708 ml) vegetable broth

1½ cups (315 g) long-grain rice

Dried cilantro (optional)

Heat the olive oil in a large deep pan over medium heat. Add the bell peppers, onion and green beans. Cook for 5 to 6 minutes. Add the okra, garlic, jalapeño, Creole seasoning, salt and pepper. Stir in the diced tomatoes, crushed tomatoes, Worcestershire sauce and vegetable broth. Bring the mixture to a boil.

Add the rice and stir to combine. Cover the pan, reduce the heat and simmer for 20 minutes.

Serve sprinkled with dried cilantro (if using).

roasted
ROOT VEGGIES & BARLEY

Hearty root vegetables are the star of the show here. Butternut squash, carrots, onions and beets are roasted to caramelized perfection, then tossed with heart-healthy barley and a delicious lemon-basil vinaigrette. Most of the cooking time in this recipe is simply waiting for the veggies to roast—giving you plenty of time to enjoy a glass of wine.

SERVES
6

3 cups (420 g) peeled and diced butternut squash (½-inch [1-cm] cubes)

1½ cups (195 g) peeled and diced carrots (½-inch [1-cm] pieces)

½ yellow onion, sliced

1 tbsp (15 ml) olive oil

1 tsp chopped fresh rosemary

Salt, to taste

Black pepper, to taste

1 (8.8-oz [250-g]) package peeled and steamed beets, cut into ½-inch (1-cm) cubes (see note)

2 cups (472 ml) vegetable broth

1 cup (200 g) barley

Chopped fresh basil (optional)

LEMON-BASIL VINAIGRETTE

1 tbsp (15 ml) olive oil

2 tbsp (30 ml) lemon juice

1 tbsp (15 ml) white wine vinegar

1 tsp Dijon mustard

1 tbsp (3 g) chopped fresh basil

Salt, to taste

Black pepper, to taste

Preheat the oven to 375°F (190°C, or gas mark 5).

In a large, ovenproof skillet, toss the butternut squash, carrots, onion, olive oil, rosemary, salt and pepper. Roast in the oven for 30 minutes, until the squash and carrots are just tender.

Remove the skillet from the oven and place it on the stovetop over medium heat. Add the beets and vegetable broth and bring to a boil. Add the barley. Reduce the heat and simmer for 15 minutes, until the barley is fully cooked.

To make the vinaigrette, in a small mixing bowl, whisk together the olive oil, lemon juice, white wine vinegar, Dijon mustard, basil, salt and pepper.

Toss the dressing with the barley and vegetables. Serve topped with additional basil (if using).

> ***note:*** This recipe calls for beets that have been pre-steamed. This makes working with them a whole lot easier, and faster. I find this little cheat helps me get dinner on the table much quicker! They can be found in the produce section of most grocery stores. If you prefer to use fresh beets, peel them, chop them, toss them with olive oil and roast them. They will take about 45 minutes to roast in the oven at 375°F (190°C, or gas mark 5). For use in this recipe, roast them for 15 minutes before adding the other vegetables to the pan.

thai
GREEN CURRY & RICE

SERVES
3

Green curry is my go-to Thai dish. It's the thing I order at every new Thai restaurant so I can "benchmark" it against all the rest. So, a lot of testing went into making this version absolutely perfect. The rice is simmered directly in the green curry broth, soaking up all the flavors of coconut, garlic and ginger. Who needs takeout when you can make dishes like this in under 30 minutes?

2 tbsp (30 ml) olive oil

½ yellow onion, sliced

2 cloves garlic, minced

1 tsp ginger paste

½ red bell pepper, sliced

½ cup (50 g) shredded carrots

⅓ cup (22 g) sliced mushrooms

1 tsp crushed red pepper flakes

½ tsp salt

3 tbsp (42 g) green curry paste

2¾ cups (650 ml) coconut milk

4 cups (944 ml) vegetable broth

½ cup (105 g) jasmine rice

¼ cup (10 g) chopped fresh cilantro (optional)

Heat the olive oil in a large pot over medium heat. Add the onion and garlic, and cook for 2 minutes. Add the ginger paste, bell pepper, carrots, mushrooms, red pepper flakes and salt. Cook for 5 to 6 minutes, until the vegetables are softened.

Add the green curry paste, coconut milk and vegetable broth. Stir to combine, and heat until the mixture begins to bubble.

Add the rice. Reduce the heat and simmer for 15 minutes.

Serve the curry topped with cilantro (if using).

note: Try swapping the green curry paste for red curry paste for a completely new—and equally delicious—dish!

indian-spiced
SWEET POTATO STEW

SERVES
6

This is one of those secretly good-for-you recipes that everyone loves to eat, without realizing it's actually a nutritional powerhouse. Protein-rich quinoa, fiber-filled chickpeas, heart-healthy sweet potatoes and superfood kale are simmered in a delicious broth infused with ginger, garlic and garam masala—the quintessential Indian spice blend. It's insanely easy and so good.

1 tbsp (15 ml) olive oil

1 yellow onion, chopped

2 cloves garlic, minced

1 tsp ginger paste

2 tsp (5 g) garam masala

2 (15.5-oz [439-g]) cans chickpeas, drained and rinsed

2 large sweet potatoes, peeled and cubed

4 cups (944 ml) vegetable broth

Salt, to taste

Black pepper, to taste

1 cup (170 g) dry quinoa, rinsed

2 cups (134 g) chopped kale

Heat the olive oil in a large pot over medium heat. Add the onion, garlic, ginger paste and garam masala. Cook for 3 to 4 minutes, until fragrant.

Add the chickpeas, sweet potatoes, vegetable broth, salt and pepper. Bring the mixture to a boil.

Add the quinoa. Reduce the heat and simmer on low for 15 minutes. Add the kale and cook for 2 minutes, until wilted.

note: This stew works equally well with rice or lentils in place of the quinoa. Just be sure to adjust the cooking time accordingly.

summery
CITRUS COUSCOUS

SERVES
4

This couscous is light and refreshing, yet filling enough for dinner. The citrus dressing is a perfect complement to the juicy oranges, creamy avocado and tangy red onions. It can be pulled together in just twenty minutes—and most of that time is just waiting for the water to boil! This couscous makes a great meal all on its own. But it's also a nice addition to your next cookout, served alongside chickpea burgers (page 46).

2 tbsp (30 ml) olive oil

4 cloves garlic, minced

3 cups (708 ml) water

1½ cups (260 g) couscous

2 avocados, peeled, pitted and chopped

2 oranges, peeled and sliced

1 red onion, thinly sliced

¼ cup (12 g) chopped fresh chives

CITRUS DRESSING

1 cup (236 ml) orange juice

2 tbsp (30 g) Dijon mustard

2 tbsp (30 ml) agave syrup

Salt, to taste

Black pepper, to taste

In a medium pot, heat the olive oil over medium-high heat. Add the garlic and cook for 2 minutes. Add the water and bring to a boil. Add the couscous and stir. Cover the pot and remove it from the heat. Let it sit undisturbed for 5 minutes.

Fluff the couscous with a fork and spread it onto a serving dish. Top the couscous with the avocados, oranges and red onion.

To make the dressing, in a small bowl, whisk together the orange juice, Dijon mustard, agave syrup, salt and pepper.

Drizzle the couscous with the dressing and top it with the chives.

balsamic
STRAWBERRY & AVOCADO QUINOA

SERVES
4

If you've never paired savory balsamic vinegar with sweet, fresh strawberries, you've been missing out on an incredible flavor match! And it gets even better when you add creamy avocado and garden-fresh herbs.

3½ cups (840 ml) water

2 cups (340 g) dry quinoa, rinsed

6 tbsp (90 ml) balsamic vinegar

¼ cup (60 ml) olive oil

Salt, to taste

Black pepper, to taste

2 cups (302 g) sliced strawberries

2 tbsp (5 g) chopped fresh mint

2 tbsp (5 g) chopped fresh parsley

¼ cup (42 g) sliced almonds

2 avocados, peeled, pitted and sliced

Pour the water into a medium pot and bring it to a boil. Add the quinoa and stir. Cover and cook for 17 minutes, or until the liquid is absorbed and the quinoa is fully cooked. Set it aside to cool.

Add the balsamic vinegar, olive oil, salt and pepper to the quinoa. Mix to combine.

Fold in the strawberries, mint and parsley. Serve topped with sliced almonds and sliced avocados.

bowls of
DELICIOUSNESS

Some evenings just call for a giant, piping hot bowl of soup. This is comfort food at its finest.

Every one of these dinner-worthy soups, stews and chilis is crafted to stand on its own as a satisfying one-pot meal. From the tangy Creamy Coconut Tomato Bisque (page 133) to the belly-warming Old-Fashioned Mushrooms and Dumplings (page 130), these recipes are full of unique flavors and hearty ingredients.

But I've gone beyond the classics here to include some of my favorite flavors from around the world too, such as the creamy African Peanut Stew (page 134) and show-stopping Vietnamese Veggie Pho (page 138).

And, of course, each one is easy to prepare in a single pot—and some of them take next to no time to make. In fact, my curried noodle soup (page 129) comes together in just fifteen minutes flat!

chickpea
COCONUT CURRY

SERVES
4

I love curry in pretty much all forms, and coconut curry has always been one of my favorites. I've married some of my most beloved Thai and Indian flavors to create this one-of-a-kind dish. It tastes like it took all day to make, but it cooks up in a single pot in under 30 minutes. Just between us—this is my favorite recipe in the book!

2 tbsp (30 ml) olive oil

1 yellow onion, chopped

2 cloves garlic, minced

1 tbsp (14 g) peeled and minced fresh ginger

1 tsp curry powder

1 cup (236 ml) vegetable broth

2 (15.5-oz [439-g]) cans chickpeas, drained and rinsed

1 (13.5-oz [400-ml]) can coconut milk

2 tbsp (28 g) red curry paste

¼ tsp chili powder (see notes)

Salt, to taste

Black pepper, to taste

Heat the oil in a high-sided pan over medium heat. Add the onion and cook for 5 to 7 minutes, until it is just slightly browned. Add the garlic, ginger and curry powder to the pan. Sauté for 1 to 2 minutes, until fragrant.

Add the vegetable broth, chickpeas, coconut milk, red curry paste and chili powder. Bring to a boil, reduce to a simmer and cook for 15 minutes. Add salt and pepper, to taste.

Serve with fresh cilantro and a slice of naan, if desired.

notes: Adjust the chili powder to your preferred spice level. I suggest adding a bit at a time and tasting until it's perfect!

Naan is a classic Indian bread that is often vegan; always check the label to be sure. You can find it in the bakery or international aisle at most grocery stores. Alternatively, you can serve the curry over prepared rice or couscous.

FOR SERVING
Fresh cilantro

Naan (optional; see notes)

15-minute
CURRIED NOODLE SOUP

SERVES
4

Those incredible Thai flavors are back one more time in this ridiculously easy one-pot noodle soup. It's infused with creamy coconut milk, spicy red curry, garlic and ginger. And yes, you really can make it in just fifteen minutes!

¼ cup (55 g) coconut oil

2 tbsp (28 g) ginger paste or minced fresh ginger

6 cloves garlic, minced

¼ cup (56 g) red curry paste

8 cups (2 L) vegetable broth

1 cup (236 ml) coconut milk, well shaken

1 (12-oz [340-g]) package rice noodles

FOR SERVING
Lime wedges

Fresh cilantro

Shredded cabbage

Heat the coconut oil in a large stockpot over medium heat. Add the ginger paste, garlic and red curry paste. Cook for 2 to 3 minutes, until fragrant.

Add the vegetable broth and coconut milk and stir. Bring the mixture to a boil. Add the rice noodles and cook for 5 minutes.

Serve with lime wedges, cilantro and shredded cabbage.

note: If you don't have rice noodles on hand, this soup works equally well with vermicelli. Just adjust the cooking time according to the package directions.

old-fashioned MUSHROOMS AND DUMPLINGS

SERVES
4

This one-pot mushrooms and dumplings dish is my plant-based answer to traditional chicken and dumplings. It's flavorful, rich, hearty and surprisingly simple. A little secret: I may have eaten this entire pot by myself. Don't tell!

2 tbsp (30 ml) olive oil

2 shallots, diced

1½ tsp (3 g) chopped fresh thyme

½ tsp salt

1 bay leaf

8 cups (2 L) vegetable broth

1.5 oz (42 g) dried shiitake mushrooms or your favorite variety

3 tbsp (45 ml) balsamic vinegar

Fresh parsley (optional)

DUMPLINGS

1 cup (125 g) all-purpose flour

1 tsp salt

½ tsp garlic powder

2 tsp (9 g) baking powder

1 tbsp (15 ml) olive oil

½ cup (120 ml) almond milk

Heat the olive oil in a large saucepan over medium heat. Add the shallots and cook for 2 to 3 minutes. Add the thyme, salt and bay leaf. Cook for 1 minute. Add the vegetable broth, dried mushrooms and balsamic vinegar. Simmer for 15 minutes.

To make the dumplings, combine the flour, salt, garlic powder, baking powder, olive oil and almond milk in a large bowl. Mix it together to form a loose batter.

Turn up the heat on the broth and allow the mixture to come to a bubble.

Roll the dumplings into large balls, roughly 1½ inches (3.5 cm), and add them to the broth. Cook for 5 to 6 minutes, turning the dumplings over halfway through the cooking time to ensure both sides get cooked evenly.

Remove the bay leaf, and serve sprinkled with parsley (if using).

creamy
COCONUT TOMATO BISQUE

There's nothing like a big bowl of tomato soup to warm up on a chilly evening—it's the ultimate comfort food. And this is one of my all-time favorite versions. The fresh ginger and creamy coconut milk add a unique twist to this belly-warming tomato soup.

2 tbsp (27 g) coconut oil

1 yellow onion, diced

2 sprigs of thyme

3 cloves garlic, minced

2 tbsp (28 g) peeled and minced fresh ginger

½ tsp salt, divided

¼ cup (66 g) tomato paste

2 tbsp (30 ml) white wine vinegar

2 (28-oz [794-g]) cans crushed tomatoes

4 cups (944 ml) vegetable broth

¼ tsp black pepper

½ cup (120 ml) canned coconut milk

¼ cup (10 g) chopped fresh cilantro

Heat the coconut oil in a large stockpot over medium-high heat. Add the onion, thyme, garlic, ginger and ¼ teaspoon of the salt. Cook, stirring often, for 3 to 4 minutes, until the onion is softened.

Add the tomato paste and cook for 1 minute. Add the white wine vinegar and cook for 1 minute.

Stir in the crushed tomatoes and the vegetable broth. Bring the mixture to a boil over high heat. Then reduce the heat to medium and simmer for 8 to 10 minutes, until thickened.

Season the bisque with the remaining salt and the pepper, adjusting to taste.

Ladle the soup into serving bowls. Shake the can of coconut milk well before opening. Use a spoon to drizzle approximately 2 tablespoons (30 ml) of coconut milk into each bowl of soup. Sprinkle each serving with cilantro to garnish.

african PEANUT STEW

SERVES
6

Peanut stew is a traditional African dish, jam-packed with incredible flavors. I've replaced the typical cabbage with super-nutritious kale for a slight twist on the original. The peanut flavor is a perfect match for tender sweet potato, and the jalapeño adds a pleasant touch of spice.

1 tbsp (15 ml) olive oil

1 onion, chopped

3 cloves garlic, minced

1 tbsp (14 g) ginger paste

½ jalapeño pepper, seeded and diced

2 tsp (5 g) cumin

¼ tsp crushed red pepper flakes

3 tbsp (48 g) tomato paste

1 large sweet potato, peeled and cubed

½ cup (129 g) peanut butter

6 cups (1.4 L) vegetable broth

1 cup (67 g) roughly chopped kale

Chopped peanuts

Heat the olive oil in a large stockpot over medium-high heat. Add the onion and cook for 3 to 4 minutes. Add the garlic, ginger paste, jalapeño, cumin, red pepper flakes and tomato paste. Stir and cook for 3 to 4 minutes.

Add the sweet potato, peanut butter and vegetable broth. Heat until the mixture comes to a boil. Reduce the heat, cover and simmer for 20 minutes, until the potatoes are tender. Add the kale and cook for 2 minutes, until it is wilted.

Serve the stew topped with chopped peanuts.

note: Try this peanut stew with the traditional shredded cabbage or protein-packed spinach in place of the kale.

cuban BLACK BEAN SOUP

SERVES
4

This authentic soup makes for a simple, filling dinner. Chunky black beans are simmered with smoky Cuban spices and loads of fresh veggies for a creamy, satisfying dish. And the whole meal can be made in a single stockpot, in under 30 minutes.

2 tbsp (30 ml) olive oil

1 yellow onion, finely diced

2 carrots, peeled and finely diced

4 cloves garlic, minced

½ serrano pepper, seeded and minced

1 tbsp (8 g) cumin

½ tsp dried oregano

¼ tsp smoked paprika

¼ tsp crushed red pepper flakes (omit for a less spicy dish)

3 (15-oz [425-g]) cans black beans, drained and rinsed

1 tomato, chopped, divided

4 cups (944 ml) vegetable broth

1 cup (154 g) fresh or frozen corn kernels

Salt, to taste

Black pepper, to taste

FOR SERVING
Fresh cilantro

Plain dairy-free yogurt

Heat the olive oil in a large stockpot over medium heat. Add the onion and carrots and cook for 7 to 8 minutes, until softened.

Add the garlic, serrano pepper, cumin, oregano, smoked paprika and red pepper flakes. Cook for 1 to 2 minutes, until fragrant.

Add half the beans and lightly mash the mixture with a potato masher or the back of a fork. Add the remaining beans, two-thirds of the chopped tomato and the vegetable broth. Bring to a bubble.

Reduce the heat and simmer for 15 minutes.

Add the corn and continue cooking for 5 minutes. Add salt and pepper, to taste.

Serve topped with the remaining diced tomato, the cilantro and a drizzle of dairy-free yogurt.

vietnamese VEGGIE PHO

Pho (pronounced "fuh") is one of the most fun dishes in the whole world. I love making a big batch of broth and noodles and letting everyone pick their own toppings. This one-pot version is brimming with delicious spice, yet it's one of the simplest recipes in this whole book! Get creative and experiment with the toppings. Try it with additions such as radishes, basil, mint, shredded carrots, bean sprouts or fresh lime wedges.

SERVES
4

2 tbsp (30 ml) olive oil

1 small onion, thinly sliced

5 oz (142 g) sliced shiitake mushrooms

2 scallions, sliced, greens and whites separated

1 tsp Chinese five-spice powder

¼ tsp crushed red pepper flakes

1 tsp ginger paste

Salt, to taste

Black pepper, to taste

6 cups (1.4 L) vegetable broth

1 (5-oz [142-g]) package rice noodles

FOR SERVING

¼ cup (10 g) alfalfa sprouts (optional)

Red chili pepper, sliced (optional)

Fresh cilantro (optional)

Hot sauce, such as Sriracha

Heat the olive oil in a large stockpot over medium heat. Add the onion, mushrooms, scallion whites, Chinese five-spice powder, red pepper flakes, ginger paste, salt and pepper. Cook for 4 to 5 minutes, until the mushrooms begin to soften.

Add the vegetable broth and bring to a boil. Add the rice noodles and simmer for 5 minutes.

Top with the sprouts, red chili pepper and cilantro (if using). Garnish with the reserved scallion greens and serve with hot sauce.

loaded
SOUTHWEST CORN
CHOWDER

SERVES
6

Did you know the word "chowder" came from a misrepresentation of the French word *chaudière,* meaning cauldron? It's thought to have been introduced to the United States by fishermen, and it's still wildly popular in the New England region today. Chowders are typically loaded with fresh seafood. Our vegan Southwestern version is brimming with corn, chunky potatoes and fresh veggies instead—all simmered in a creamy broth. If you can find farm-fresh corn at your farmers' market, it really adds something special to this dish!

1 tbsp (15 ml) olive oil

1 yellow onion, diced

1 red bell pepper, diced

1 carrot, peeled and diced

1 serrano pepper, seeded and finely diced (omit for a less spicy dish)

2 cloves garlic, minced

¼ cup (31 g) all-purpose flour

5 cups (1.2 L) vegetable broth

1 lb (454 g) Yukon Gold potatoes, diced

4 cups (616 g) fresh or frozen corn kernels

¼ tsp smoked paprika

¼ tsp dried thyme

Salt, to taste

Black pepper, to taste

⅔ cup (157 ml) almond milk

FOR SERVING (OPTIONAL)
Chopped fresh chives

Chopped fresh parsley

Heat the olive oil in a large stockpot over medium heat. Add the onion, bell pepper, carrot and serrano pepper. Cook for 7 to 8 minutes, until softened. Add the garlic and flour. Cook for 1 minute, stirring continually. Slowly stir in the vegetable broth, so the flour is fully combined with the broth.

Add the potatoes, corn, smoked paprika, thyme, salt and pepper. Bring to a boil. Reduce the heat and simmer for 20 to 25 minutes, until the potatoes are tender.

Add the almond milk. Stir and cook for 2 to 3 minutes, until heated through. Serve the chowder topped with chives and parsley (if using).

balsamic
FRENCH ONION SOUP

SERVES
4

French onion soup was one of my favorite dishes as a kid, and one of the first things I missed after going veggie. This veganized version brings all the flavor of the original in an easy one-pot recipe. Sweet caramelized onions are simmered in a flavorful broth, then topped with crusty bread and bubbly melted "cheese."

2 tbsp (30 ml) olive oil

4 yellow onions, thinly sliced

3 cloves garlic, minced

2 bay leaves

2 sprigs of thyme

1½ cups (354 ml) white wine, such as Chardonnay

6 cups (1.4 L) vegetable broth

¼ cup (60 ml) balsamic vinegar

Salt, to taste

Black pepper, to taste

4 slices baguette

1 cup (121 g) vegan mozzarella cheese shreds

Preheat the oven to 350°F (175°C, or gas mark 4).

Heat the olive oil in a large stockpot over medium-low heat. Add the onions and cook slowly for 15 to 20 minutes, stirring often, until they are lightly caramelized. Add the garlic, bay leaves and thyme. Cook for 1 minute. Add the white wine and cook for 5 to 7 minutes, until slightly reduced. Add the vegetable broth and bring to a boil. Reduce the heat and simmer for 20 minutes.

Add the balsamic vinegar and stir. Remove the bay leaves. Add salt and pepper, to taste.

Spoon the soup into four ovenproof serving dishes. Top each bowl with a slice of baguette, and sprinkle with ¼ cup (30 g) of the vegan cheese shreds. Place the bowls in the oven for 3 to 5 minutes, until the vegan cheese is melted and the baguette is slightly toasted.

smoky
WHITE BEAN CHILI

There's nothing better than cozying up with a big bowl of chili on a rainy night. I love chili in pretty much all forms. This vegan version features chunky white beans for the base, lots of colorful veggies and smoky poblano peppers. This is an easy, protein-rich dish that the entire family will enjoy.

2 tbsp (30 ml) olive oil

1 yellow onion, chopped

2 cloves garlic, minced

3 carrots, peeled and diced

1 poblano pepper, seeded and minced

2 (15.5-oz [439-g]) cans cannellini beans, drained and rinsed

2 cups (472 ml) vegetable broth

1 tsp salt

1 tsp cumin

1 tsp dried oregano

½ tsp black pepper

¼ tsp smoked paprika

½ cup (120 ml) almond milk

1 tbsp (8 g) cornstarch

1 cup (40 g) chopped fresh spinach

FOR SERVING
Sliced scallions

Sliced red onion

Sliced avocado

Heat the olive oil in a large stockpot over medium heat. Add the onion, garlic, carrots and poblano pepper. Cook for 6 to 8 minutes, until the carrots are beginning to soften.

Add the beans, vegetable broth, salt, cumin, oregano, pepper and smoked paprika. Stir and cook for 2 minutes. Add the almond milk and cornstarch. Stir. Bring the mixture to a boil.

Reduce the heat and simmer for 10 to 15 minutes, until the chili is thickened. Stir in the spinach and cook for 2 minutes, until it is wilted.

Serve with scallions, red onion and avocado.

EDAMAME MISO SOUP

Edamame steals the show in this creative take on traditional miso soup. White miso brings that distinct umami flavor to this one-pot soup. It's delicious, filling and lots of fun to eat. Try experimenting with different toppings and letting the whole family build their own bowls.

SERVES
4

1 tbsp (15 ml) olive oil

½ yellow onion, chopped

1 red bell pepper, sliced

1 tbsp (14 g) ginger paste

2 cloves garlic, minced

6 cups (1.4 L) vegetable broth

3 tbsp (72 g) white miso paste (see note)

¼ cup (28 g) shredded carrots

1 (10-oz [280-g]) package frozen edamame, shelled

Salt, to taste

Black pepper, to taste

FOR SERVING

2 radishes, sliced

2 scallions, sliced

¼ cup (18 g) shredded cabbage

Heat the olive oil in a large stockpot over medium heat. Add the onion, bell pepper, ginger paste and garlic. Cook for 4 to 5 minutes, until the vegetables are softened.

Add the vegetable broth, miso paste, carrots and edamame. Bring the mixture to a boil. Reduce the heat and simmer for 5 minutes. Season to taste with salt and pepper.

Serve the soup topped with radishes, scallions and shredded cabbage.

note: White miso is made primarily from soybeans and rice, and it is naturally vegan. However, some manufacturers add ingredients such as bonito flakes, so it's always a good idea to double-check the label.

rise
AND SHINE

We have a long-standing tradition of cooking a big family breakfast on the weekends. It's something we all love, but simply don't have time for during the workweek.

So, we indulge on the weekends. But you can do the same, without a lot of fuss, any time of the week using these easy one-pan breakfast recipes.

If you're looking for something traditional, try out the Crispy Breakfast Hash (page 154) or the decadent Vanilla-Maple French Toast Bake (page 150). And if you're ready to mix things up, go straight for the Savory Mushroom Congee (page 153)—an incredible rice-based dish commonly eaten throughout Asia.

With all of these plant-based breakfasts at the ready, you'll never miss bacon and eggs again!

vanilla-maple
FRENCH TOAST BAKE

SERVES
6

This easy one-pan casserole tastes exactly like traditional French toast, but it's 100 percent vegan and a lot less work! You can even prepare this the night before and pop it in the oven in the morning. My son asked for seconds of this one, then ate it again for lunch the same day. I call that a win!

CASSEROLE

4 cups (140 g) cubed baguette

¼ cup (60 ml) melted coconut oil

1 cup (236 ml) almond milk

1 tsp vanilla extract

½ tsp cinnamon

¼ tsp salt

¼ cup (60 ml) maple syrup, plus more for serving

CRUMBLE TOPPING

⅓ cup (73 g) room-temperature coconut oil

½ cup (40 g) quick-cooking oats

⅓ cup (73 g) packed brown sugar

Preheat the oven to 350°F (175°C, or gas mark 4).

To make the casserole, in a large baking dish, mix together the baguette cubes, coconut oil, almond milk, vanilla, cinnamon, salt and maple syrup. Bake for 15 minutes.

Meanwhile, to make the crumble topping, in a small bowl, mix together the coconut oil, oats and brown sugar. Set the topping aside.

After 15 minutes, remove the casserole from the oven and sprinkle the crumble topping over the top. Return the casserole to the oven and bake for 15 minutes more.

Serve with extra maple syrup.

savory
MUSHROOM CONGEE

SERVES
4

Who says breakfast has to be sweet? Congee is a savory rice dish served for breakfast in many Asian countries. It's extremely versatile, pairing well with all kinds of creative toppings. Experiment with your favorites for an endless variety of dishes. Some vegan-friendly ideas are scallions, crispy fried onions, cilantro, hot chili oil or roasted butternut squash.

1 tbsp (15 ml) olive oil

1 shallot, finely chopped

1 tbsp (14 g) minced fresh ginger

1½ cups (100 g) sliced mushrooms, any variety

1½ cups (354 ml) water

¾ cup (158 g) brown rice

3 tbsp (45 ml) soy sauce

FOR SERVING

2 tsp (10 ml) sesame oil

2 tsp (7 g) black sesame seeds

2 tbsp (6 g) chopped fresh chives

Heat the olive oil over medium heat in a medium pot. Add the shallot and ginger and cook for 2 to 3 minutes. Add the mushrooms and cook for 4 to 5 minutes, until softened.

Add the water and bring to a boil. Add the rice. Reduce the heat and simmer for 40 minutes, or until the rice is tender and the liquid is fully absorbed. Stir in the soy sauce.

Divide the congee into serving bowls. Drizzle with sesame oil. Sprinkle with black sesame seeds and chives.

crispy BREAKFAST HASH

We love big, hearty breakfasts. But I don't love spending all morning in the kitchen, especially with a hungry kid waiting. This simple and filling one-skillet meal comes together easily with items I already have in my pantry!

2 tbsp (30 ml) olive oil

1 green bell pepper, seeded and chopped

1 red onion, chopped

3 cups (600 g) frozen diced potatoes

¼ tsp chili powder

½ tsp cumin

¼ tsp salt

½ tsp garlic powder

1 (15-oz [425-g]) can black beans, drained and rinsed

Dried cilantro

YOGURT SAUCE

½ cup (120 g) plain dairy-free yogurt

1 tbsp (15 ml) lemon juice

1 tbsp (2 g) dried cilantro

Heat the olive oil in a large nonstick skillet over medium heat. Add the bell pepper and red onion. Cook for 4 to 5 minutes, until softened.

Add the potatoes, chili powder, cumin, salt and garlic powder. Stir. Cook for 15 to 17 minutes, stirring occasionally, until the potatoes are heated through. Add the black beans and cook for 2 to 3 minutes, until warm.

To make the sauce, mix together the dairy-free yogurt, lemon juice and cilantro in a small bowl.

Serve the breakfast hash with a drizzle of the cilantro-yogurt sauce and extra cilantro for garnish.

CHAI-SPICED OATMEAL

Take that traditional oatmeal up a few notches by simmering it in a delicious chai-spiced almond milk. It's rich, creamy and tastes totally decadent. But it's actually a nutritious breakfast that's easy to throw together in a single pot. And it only takes about fifteen minutes from start to finish!

**SERVES
4**

¼ cup (55 g) coconut oil

1 tsp cinnamon

½ tsp nutmeg

½ tsp ground ginger

½ tsp allspice

½ tsp salt

½ cup (110 g) packed brown sugar, plus more for serving

6 cups (1.4 L) almond milk

1 tsp vanilla extract

2 cups (160 g) quick-cooking oats

FOR SERVING

½ cup (59 g) chopped walnuts

12 strawberries, sliced

20 raspberries

¼ cup (23 g) shredded coconut

Heat the coconut oil in a medium pot over medium heat. Add the cinnamon, nutmeg, ground ginger, allspice, salt and brown sugar. Stir for 30 seconds, until fragrant.

Add the almond milk and vanilla. Bring the mixture to a bubble. Add the oats. Reduce the heat and simmer for 5 to 7 minutes, until the liquid is absorbed and the oats are tender.

Sprinkle with walnuts, berries and coconut. Serve with extra brown sugar, if desired.

> *note:* Try topping with blueberries, granola or even dark chocolate chips for a new spin on this recipe.

strawberry-ginger
BISCUIT PIE

Fresh biscuits are irresistibly good, but they can be hard to prepare without special biscuit cutters and a ton of time. So, I created this one-pan biscuit pie as an alternative. It has all the incredible goodness of homemade biscuits, infused with ginger and fresh strawberries, and cooked up in a single skillet.

SERVES
4

½ cup (120 ml) almond milk

1 tbsp (15 ml) white wine vinegar

2 tbsp (28 g) baking powder

½ tsp salt

1 tsp sugar

¼ cup (60 ml) melted coconut oil

1 tsp ginger paste

1 cup (151 g) sliced strawberries

Strawberry jam

Preheat the oven to 425°F (220°C, or gas mark 7).

In a large bowl, mix together the almond milk, white wine vinegar, baking powder, salt, sugar, coconut oil, ginger paste and strawberries. Pour the batter into a 10-inch (25-cm) ovenproof skillet.

Bake for 25 minutes, until just golden. Serve with the strawberry jam.

note: Try this recipe with blueberries in place of the strawberries for a completely new dish.

simply sweet
ONE-POT
TREATS

No meal is complete without a little bite of something sweet, so I couldn't resist including a few of my favorite desserts in this cookbook.

From a kid-friendly Chocolate-Espresso Skillet Cake (page 165) to grown-up Boozy Coconut Bananas Foster (page 162), there's something to please every sweet tooth. And you'd never guess these rich, creamy flavors were created without a drop of dairy.

These vegan treats feel incredibly indulgent, yet they're all simple to prepare in a single pot or skillet. So there's no excuse for skipping dessert!

boozy
COCONUT BANANAS FOSTER

This boozy bananas Foster is the perfect sweet treat—fresh bananas are caramelized in coconut oil, dark rum and brown sugar. It's an indulgent dessert that takes just fifteen minutes and a single pot to pull together! Serve it up with ice-cold dairy-free vanilla ice cream. This is the perfect sweet ending for a date-night dinner.

SERVES
2

¼ cup (55 g) coconut oil

⅔ cup (145 g) packed brown sugar

3 oz (88 ml) dark rum

1 tsp vanilla extract

½ tsp cinnamon

3 bananas, sliced lengthwise into 2-inch (5-cm) pieces

FOR SERVING (OPTIONAL)
Coconut flakes

Chopped nuts

Dairy-free vanilla ice cream (see note)

Melt the coconut oil in a large skillet over medium heat. Add the sugar, rum, vanilla and cinnamon. Stir. Bring to a bubble. Add the bananas and gently toss with the rum sauce to coat. Cook for 2 to 3 minutes, until the bananas are hot.

Sprinkle with coconut flakes and chopped nuts (if using). Serve with dairy-free vanilla ice cream (if using).

note: You'll find an incredible variety of dairy-free ice creams and sorbets available today. So Delicious is one of my favorite brands!

chocolate-espresso
SKILLET CAKE

Skillet cakes are fun to make, and I had a blast creating this one with my son. The cake batter mixes up quickly in a single bowl, then you simply bake and serve the cake straight from the skillet. Yum!

SERVES
8

Olive oil cooking spray

2 cups (250 g) all-purpose flour

1 cup (192 g) sugar

1 tsp salt

1 tsp baking powder

¼ cup (22 g) cocoa powder

¾ cup (177 ml) almond milk

1 tbsp (6 g) espresso powder or instant coffee

⅓ cup (80 ml) olive oil

1½ tsp (8 ml) vanilla extract

1 tbsp (15 ml) white wine vinegar

TOPPINGS (OPTIONAL)
Chocolate syrup

Fresh berries

Whipped coconut cream (page 170)

Dairy-free ice cream

Preheat the oven to 350°F (175°C, or gas mark 4). Coat a 12-inch (30-cm) skillet with olive oil cooking spray.

In a large bowl, add the flour, sugar, salt, baking powder, cocoa powder, almond milk, espresso powder, olive oil, vanilla and white wine vinegar. Mix to form a cake batter. Pour the batter into the skillet.

Bake in the oven for approximately 25 minutes. The cake is done when a sharp knife inserted into the center comes out clean. Remove the cake from the oven and allow it to cool to room temperature.

Serve with your favorite toppings, such as chocolate syrup, fresh berries, whipped coconut cream or dairy-free ice cream.

skillet
BERRY COBBLER

This simple skillet cobbler is so easy to throw together. Fresh berries are stewed in brown sugar and baking spices, then topped with a crumbly cobbler crust and baked to a bubbly golden finish.

1½ lbs (680 g) strawberries, hulled and sliced in half

9 oz (255 g) blackberries

9 oz (255 g) raspberries

¾ cup (143 g) sugar, divided

¼ cup (55 g) packed brown sugar

¼ tsp cardamom

¼ tsp ground cinnamon

1 tsp lemon juice

1 tsp vanilla extract

¼ tsp plus ⅛ tsp salt, divided

1 tbsp (8 g) cornstarch

1½ cups (188 g) all-purpose flour

¾ cup (165 g) coconut oil

Heat a large skillet over medium-high heat. Add the strawberries, blackberries, raspberries, ¼ cup (48 g) of the sugar, brown sugar, cardamom, cinnamon, lemon juice, vanilla, ⅛ teaspoon of salt and the cornstarch. Stir to combine.

Cook for 8 to 10 minutes, until the mixture is hot and beginning to bubble.

In a medium bowl, combine the flour, remaining ½ cup (95 g) of sugar, ¼ teaspoon of salt and the coconut oil. It should form a loose dough.

Roll the dough into disks, roughly 2 inches (5 cm) wide, and arrange them on top of the berry mixture. Don't worry if it looks messy!

Bake the cobbler for 30 to 35 minutes, until it is golden and crispy. Let it cool to a safe temperature before serving.

> *note:* I use regular cane sugar and brown sugar throughout this book. Depending on where you live and the brands you have access to, your sugar may be processed with bone char—making it decidedly not vegan. Choose an organic brand and be sure to check the label to ensure it's a vegan-friendly variety.

gingered
CARROT HALWA

Halwa is an incredibly delicious carrot-based pudding commonly found in India. The traditional version involves a ton of milk and ghee to deliver the indulgent creamy consistency. This veganized version is every bit as delicious as the original, but a bit lighter thanks to its dairy-free nature. I think that means you can eat twice as much. You can easily scale up this recipe if you're serving a larger group. Dig in!

**SERVES
2**

¼ cup (55 g) coconut oil, divided

4 cups (440 g) shredded carrots

1 tbsp (14 g) ginger paste or minced fresh ginger

3 cups (708 ml) almond milk

¼ cup (55 g) packed brown sugar

1 tbsp (8 g) cardamom

¼ cup (27 g) sliced almonds, divided

2 tbsp (10 g) coconut flakes

Heat 3 tablespoons (41 g) of the coconut oil in a medium pot over medium heat. Add the carrots and ginger paste. Cook for 10 to 12 minutes, until the coconut oil is fully absorbed into the carrots.

Add the almond milk. Cook, stirring occasionally, for 35 minutes, until milk is fully absorbed.

Add the brown sugar, 1 tablespoon (14 g) of coconut oil, cardamom and 2 tablespoons (14 g) of the almonds. Cook for 5 minutes.

Garnish the halwa with the remaining sliced almonds and the coconut flakes.

baked apples with
WHIPPED COCONUT CREAM

SERVES
4

Baked apples are one of those nostalgic childhood favorites that no one can resist. This one-pan version is made even more delicious when topped with a homemade whipped coconut cream. You won't believe how simple this is to pull together.

8 apples, cored and sliced

¼ cup (60 ml) melted coconut oil

1 tbsp (6 g) allspice

½ cup (110 g) packed brown sugar

¼ cup (60 ml) lemon juice

2 tsp (6 g) cornstarch

WHIPPED COCONUT CREAM
2 (14-oz [397-g]) cans chilled coconut cream (not shaken; see note)

¼ cup (48 g) sugar

Preheat the oven to 350°F (175°C, or gas mark 4).

In a 9 x 13-inch (23 x 33-cm) baking dish, mix together the apples, coconut oil, allspice, brown sugar, lemon juice and cornstarch. Bake for 30 minutes, until the apples are soft and caramelized.

To make the whipped coconut cream, open the can of coconut cream and carefully scoop just the solids into a small mixing bowl. Use a whisk to beat the coconut cream until soft peaks form. Add the sugar, and whisk for another minute to incorporate. You can also use an electric mixer for this task, if you prefer.

Serve the apples in individual bowls, topped with a dollop of whipped coconut cream.

> *note:* Coconut milk and coconut cream are *not* the same ingredient. Coconut cream has a much thicker, richer consistency. If you have the time, put the can of coconut cream in the fridge for a few hours or overnight. It will be easier to whip!

ACKNOWLEDGMENTS

My most heartfelt thanks go out to everyone that made this book possible.

Thank you to my parents, Candie and Dave, for encouraging my vegetarianism from an early age, when many other parents would have shut it down.

Thank you to my wonderful mother-in-law, Anita, for helping me cook the very first recipes in this book. Getting started is the hardest part!

Thank you to my incredibly patient husband, Akrit, and incredibly cool kid, Ayan, for taste testing all 75 of these dishes and putting up with a gigantic mess in our kitchen for many months.

Thank you to Page Street Publishing for taking a chance on my very first cookbook, and to their wonderful team for bringing it to life.

And most of all, thank you to my amazing readers for sharing their cooking and their lives with me every day.

ABOUT THE AUTHOR

Nicole is the cook and author behind Delicious Everyday, where she shares her vegetarian and vegan creations with the world. As a twenty-five-year vegetarian, she knows that meatless meals go way beyond salads and tofu. So she strives to craft delicious recipes that show the world how easy and delicious it can be to "go veggie."

When she's not busy cooking up new creations, Nicole is an avid photographer, a busy mom and an entrepreneurial businesswoman.

She lives in sunny Florida with her husband, son and their big goofy dog.

TO SEE WHAT SHE'S COOKING NEXT, BE SURE TO FOLLOW HER AT
Website: www.DeliciousEveryday.com
Instagram: www.instagram.com/deliciouseveryday
Facebook: www.facebook.com/deliciouseveryday
Facebook Group: www.facebook.com/groups/deliciouseveryday
Pinterest: www.pinterest.com/deliciouseveryday

INDEX